Emily Sarah Holt

Mistress Margery

A Tale of the Lollards

Emily Sarah Holt

Mistress Margery
A Tale of the Lollards

ISBN/EAN: 9783337026745

Printed in Europe, USA, Canada, Australia, Japan

Cover: Foto ©Thomas Meinert / pixelio.de

More available books at **www.hansebooks.com**

Mistress Margery

A Tale of the Lollards

BY

EMILY SARAH HOLT

AUTHOR OF

"Sister Rose," "Ashcliffe Hall," "Margery's Son," etc.

" I fear no harm, with Thee at hand to bless;
 Life hath no ills, and death no bitterness.
 Where, Death, thy sting? Where, Grave, thy victory?
 I triumph still, if Thou abide with me."
                            —REV. H. F. LYTE.

NEW EDITION

John F. Shaw & Co., Ltd.,

3, Pilgrim Street, London, E.C.

PREFACE.

THE principal historical characters who appear in this story are Sastre and Archbishop Arundel. William Sastre (also called Sawtre) was originally a parish priest in London. Though for many years he was a fearless and uncompromising preacher of the truth (so far as he knew it), yet, when tried, Sastre at first exhibited that timidity which appears to have been one of the chief failings of Wycliffe himself. "When persecution arose, he was offended." He formally recanted before the Bishop of Norwich the opinions which he had maintained and preached so faithfully before. But Sastre—like Cranmer, two hundred years later—bitterly mourned his criminal weakness. After his recantation, he gave such offence to the Council by again preaching the doctrines of grace, that he was once more brought before them; and this time he continued faithful unto death, which he suffered on the 26th of February, 1401.

Archbishop Arundel was that bitterest of all per-secutors—a renegade. His own mind had at one time been impressed with Lollard views; but his after conduct renders it evident that these doctrines had merely occupied his intellect, without in any respect influencing his heart. In 1394, when he was Archbishop of York, we find Arundel preaching a funeral sermon for Queen Anne of Bohemia, in which he highly commended her conduct in constantly reading the Bible in English. The Queen possessed four English translations, which she had laid before Arundel, and had requested his judgment as to their respective fidelity. Arundel's reply was, that no fault could be found with any of them. Yet no sooner was this prelate raised to the See of Canterbury, within a very short period after he preached this sermon, than he enlisted himself, heart and soul, on the side of the persecution, and was, indeed, its moving cause and its principal abettor.

The Lollard persecution raged fiercely through the whole reign of Henry V., and may be said to have reached its height with the martyrdom of Lord Cobham, who was an attendant and personal friend of the King. This admirable man suffered in 1417. During the minority of Henry VI., two or three cases of persecution occur; but this gentle King, "the holy Henry," was not likely to lend himself to any butchering of men for their faith's sake. The last instance of a Lollard martyr occurs in the reign of Henry VIII. Seven years after this, broke the first dawn of the glorious Reformation; and the few Lollards who remained are not thenceforth to be distinguished from the later Reformers.

It seems almost surprising that so little information should have descended to us regarding these noble confessors of Christ, of whom unquestionably Lord Cobham was the most enlightened and most fearless. Wycliffe himself appears to have been still involved in darkness upon many points. He believed in Purgatory, and it seems doubtful whether he did not sometimes pray to the Virgin. He mixed himself up far too much with politics, and contented himself with denouncing Popish abuses, rather than providing the antidote. Still, after all, let us remember how much he had to contend with, and how much he did for England in presenting her with the first translation of Scripture into the vulgar tongue. Whatever were the failings of him who has been called " the Morning Star of the Reformation," he was still a mighty instrument in God's hand, a great confessor of God's truth, and, there seems no reason to doubt, a true child of God. And what is the greatest man who ever lived, whether king, statesman, hero, or martyr, but a tool in the hand of Him who ordereth all things according to the counsel of His own will !

I have in the ensuing pages, in charity to my readers, avoided shocking their sensibilities with the worst features of a Romish persecution. The stake, however, was in reality only the end of a long previous martyrdom. The rack, the pulleys, and all the numberless and nameless instruments employed by the craft and subtilty of the devil or man for the torture of God's saints, have been carefully kept out of sight in these pages—not because they did not exist, nor with the least view to conceal the iniquity of her who is " drunk with the blood of the martyrs of Jesus," but simply from a desire to spare the feelings of my readers.

Six men and one woman were burned in the reign of Henry IV., *for teaching their children the Lord's Prayer and the Ten Commandments in English*. A most instructive comment on this fact is the celebrated sentence in the canon law of Rome, which then prevailed in the Church of England—" THE CHURCH NEVER HAS CHANGED, NOR CAN CHANGE ! "

CONTENTS

CHAPTER I.

" Give me the book, and let me read ;
My soul is strangely stirred—
They are such words of love and truth
As ne'er before I heard ! "
—MARY HOWITT.

THE sun was shining brightly on the battlements and casements of Lovell Tower. The season was spring, and the year 1395. Within the house, though it was barely seven o'clock in the morning, all was bustle and confusion, for Dame Lovell was superintending her handmaidens in the preparation of dinner. A buxom woman was Dame Lovell, neither tall nor short, but decidedly stout, with a round, good-natured face, which just then glowed and burned under the influence of the fire roaring on the large grateless hearth. She wore a black dress, heavily trimmed at the bottom with fur, and she carried on her head one of those remarkable elevations generally known as the Syrian or conical head-dress, made of black stiffened gauze, and spangled with

11

golden stars. Her assistants, mostly girls of from sixteen to twenty-five years of age, were occupied in various parts of the kitchen; while Mistress Katherine, a staid-looking woman of middle age, who filled a post somewhat similar to the modern one of housekeeper, was employed at a side table in mixing some particularly elaborate compound. Among this busy throng moved Dame Lovell, now giving a stir to a pot, and now peeping into a pan, boxing the ears of any maiden who appeared remiss in her duty, and generally keeping up a strict and active supervision.

"Nan, thy leeks be not hewn small enough. Cicely, look to the pottage, that it boil not over. Al'ce, thou idle jade!"—with a sound box on the ear,— "thou hast left out the onions in thy blanch-porre! Margery! Madge! Why, Madge, I say! Where is Mistress Margery, maidens? Joan, lass, hie thee up, and see whether Mistress Margery be not in the chamber."

Joan, a diminutive girl of sixteen, quitted the parsley she was chopping, and ran lithely out of the room, to which she soon returned, and, dropping a courtesy, announced that "Mistress Margery was in her chamber, and was coming presently,"—which latter word, in the year 1395, meant not " by and by," as it now does, but " at present." Mistress Margery verified the assertion of Joan by following her into the kitchen almost immediately. And since Mistress Margery is to play the important part of heroine, it may be well to devote a few words to her person and costume.

She is the only child of Sir Geoffrey Lovell, Knight, and Dame Agnes Lovell, and is now seventeen years of age ; rather under the middle height, slenderly formed, with an appearance of great fragility and delicacy ; her complexion is very fair, of that extreme fairness which often betokens disease, and her face almost colourless. Her features are regular, and classical in their contour ; her eyes are a clear gray —honest, truthful eyes, that look straight at you ; and her hair, which is almost long enough, when let down, to touch her feet, is of that pale golden colour so much celebrated in the Middle Ages, and so very rarely to be seen now. Mistress Margery's attire comprises a black dress, so stiff, partly from its own richness of material, and partly with whalebone, that it is quite capable of standing upright without any assistance from Mistress Margery's person. Its trimming consists of a border of gris, or marten's fur ; and over this black petticoat the young lady wears a côte-hardie, or close-fitting jacket, also edged with gris. Her head is not encumbered by the steeple-cap which disfigures her mother; instead of it she wears the beautiful "dove-cote," a net of golden tissue, ornamented with pearls, within which her hair is confined.

It may also be as well to notice here, that Mistress Margery is highly accomplished. Of course she can play the lute, and sing, and work elaborate and delicate embroidery, and compound savoury dishes; and equally of course does she know any nobleman or gentleman by a glance at his shield, and can tell you in a moment to whom belong the three lions rampant sable, and who owns the bend engrailed argent on a field gules. These are but the ordinary acquirements of a gentlewoman; but our heroine knows more than this. Mistress Margery can read; and the hand-maidens furthermore whisper to each other, with profound admiration of their young mistress's extraordinary knowledge, that Mistress Margery can *write*. Dame Lovell cannot do either; but Sir Geoffrey, who is a literary man, and possesses a library, has determined that his daughter shall receive a first-rate education. Sir Geoffrey's library is a very large one, for it consists of no less than forty-two volumes, five of which are costly illuminated manuscripts, and consist of the Quest of the Sangraal,[1] the Travels of Sir John Maundeville, the Chronicle of Matthew Paris, Saint Augustine's City of God, and a Breviary. Dame Lovell has no Breviary, and as she could not read it if she had, does not require one; but Margery, having obtained her father's permission to do so, has employed her powers of writing and illuminating in making an elaborate copy of his Breviary for her own use; and from an illumination in this book, not quite finished, representing Judas Iscariot in parti-coloured stockings, and Saint Peter shooting at Malchus with a cross-bow, is Margery now summoned away to the kitchen.

Margery entered the kitchen with a noiseless step, and making a low courtesy to her mother, said, in a remarkably clear, silvery voice, " It pleased you to send for me, good mother."

"Yea, lass; give a hand to the blanch-porre, for Al'ce knows no more than my shoe; and then see

---

[1] The Sangraal was the vessel in which the wine was contained which Christ gave to His disciples, saying, " Drink ye all of this ; " this vessel was supposed to have been brought into England by Joseph of Arimathea ; and the " quest " or search for this important relic formed one of the chief adventures of the Knights of the Round Table.

to the grewall, whilst I scrape these almonds for the almond butter."

Margery quietly performed her task, and spoke to the mortified Al'ce in a much gentler tone than Dame Lovell had done. She was occupied in the preparation of "eels in grewall," a kind of eel-stew, when a slender youth, a little older than herself, and attired in the usual costume of a page, entered the kitchen.

" Why, Richard Pynson ! " cried Dame Lovell, " thou art a speedy messenger, in good sooth. I looked not for thee until evensong."

" I finished mine errand, good mistress," replied the youth, " earlier by much than I looked for to do."

" Hast heard any news, Richard ? "

" None, mistress mine, unless it be news that a homily will be preached in Bostock Church on Sunday next ensuing, by a regular of Oxenforde, one Master Sastre."

The grewall was standing still, and Margery was listening intently to the words of Richard Pynson, as he carelessly leaned against the wall.

" Will you go, Mistress Margery ? "

Margery looked timidly at her mother. " I would like well to go," said she, " an' it might stand with your good pleasure."

"Ay, lass, go," replied Dame Lovell, good-naturedly. "It is seldom we have a homily in Bostock Church. Parson Leggatt is not much given to preaching, meseemeth."

"I will go with you, Master Pynson," said Margery, resuming the concoction of the dainty dish before her, "with a very good will, for I should like greatly to hear the Reverend Father. I never yet heard preach a scholar of Oxenforde."

Dame Lovell moved away to take the pottage off the fire, and Pynson, approaching Margery, whispered to her, "They say that this Master Sastre preacheth strange things, like as did Master John Wycliffe a while agone; howbeit, since Holy Church interfereth not, I trow we may well go to hear him."

Margery's colour rose, and she said in a low voice, "It will do us no harm, trow?"

"I trust not so," answered Richard; and, taking up his hunting-bag, he quitted the room.

"Why, Cicely!" exclaimed Dame Lovell, turning round from the pottage, "had I wist thou hadst put no saffron herein, thou shouldst have had mine hand about thine ears, lass! Bring the saffron presently! No saffron, quotha!"

Before we accompany Margery and Richard to

hear the homily of Master Sastre, it might perhaps
be as well to prevent any misunderstanding on the
part of the reader with respect to Richard Pynson.
He is the page of Sir Geoffrey Lovell, and the son of
Sir John Pynson of Pynsonlee ; for in the year 1395,
wherein our story opens, it is the custom for young
gentlemen, even the sons of peers, to be educated as
page or squire to some neighbouring knight of wealth
and respectability.   Richard Pynson, therefore, though
he may seem to occupy a subordinate position, is
in every respect the equal of Margery.

The morning on which Master Sastre was to deliver
his homily was one of those delicious spring days
which seem the immediate harbingers of summer.
Margery, in her black dress, and with a warm hood
over her côte-hardie, was assisted by her father to
mount her pillion, Richard Pynson being already
seated before her on the gray palfrey : for in the days
of pillions, if the gentleman assisted the lady on her
pillion *before* he mounted himself, he ran imminent
risk of knocking her off when he should attempt to
mount.   They rode leisurely to church, the distance
being about two miles, and a little foot-page ran beside
them charged with the care of the palfrey, while they
attended the service.   Mass was performed by the

parish priest, but the scholar from Oxford, who sat in the sedilia, where Margery could scarcely see him, took no part in the service beyond reading the Gospel.

The sermons of that day, as a rule, may be spoken of in two classes. Either the preacher would read a passage of Scripture in Latin, and throw in here and there a few remarks by way of commentary, or else the sermon was a long and dry disquisition upon some of the (frequently very absurd) dogmas of the schoolmen ; such as, whether angels were synonymous with spirits, which of the seven principal angels was the chief, how long it took Gabriel to fly from heaven to earth at the Annunciation, at what time of day he appeared, how he was dressed, &c. Sastre's discourse could not be comprised in either of these classes. He read his text first, as usual, in Latin, but then he said :

" And now, brethren and sistren, to declare in the vulgar tongue unto you that have not the tongues, this passage of God's Word as sueth.[1] '*The Lombe that was slayn is worthi to take vertue and Godhed and wisdom and strengthe and onour and glorie and blessyng !* '"[2]

---

[1] Follows.

[2] It will readily be seen that all the quotations from Scripture in this story are necessarily taken from Wycliffe's translation.

What followed was no scholastic disquisition, no common-place remarks on the passage chosen. "The Lamb that was slain" was the beginning and the end of Sastre's discourse. He divided his sermon into the following subjects. "Who is the Lamb?—how and why was He slain?—why is He worthy?—and, who are the speakers in the text who thus proclaim His worthiness?" He showed them, by a reference to the Mosaic sacrifices, why Christ was called a Lamb; he told them most fully that He died, the Just for the unjust, that He might bring us to God; he placed completely before his audience the full and free and finished nature of His perfect work: he told them that God's love to sinners was such that He gave out of His bosom His own dear Son, the Son of His love, that their sins might be counted His, and that His righteousness might be accounted theirs. And under his last head, he spoke of that holy, happy city whereinto no sin, nor harm, nor death could ever enter; whose foundations were gems, and whose gates pearls; the dwelling-place of the blessed ones, who having washed their robes, and made them white in the blood of the Lamb, would never rest day nor night in singing the praises of His worthiness.

Sastre also drew the attention of his hearers to

the fact that the ascription of praise in the text was made by the angels. "In all this Book," remarked he, "I find nowhere such like laud as this given unto any but God only. The blessed angels do worship unto the Lamb, but I see not any offer for to do worship unto the angels, save only Saint John himself, who doth twice fall down to worship afore the feet of the angel which did show these things unto him. But I find not the angel in any wise gladded with the same. Nay, the blessed John doth receive a sharp rebuking of his folly : 'See thou that thou do not,' saith the angel ; 'worschipe thou God.' Wherefore, good friends, ye may see hence how foolish are they who do worship unto the blessed angels : and how grievous would be the same unto those good spirits of God if they did knowledge it. Whether or no they be witting of such matters, I wis not, for this Book saith nought thereupon ; but ye see, friends, that if they wit it, it doth anger them ; and if they wit it not, what are ye the better for praying unto them ? Moreover, meseemeth for the same reason, that the blessed Virgin Saint Mary, who is now in heaven with her Son and Lord, Christ, would not be in any wise over well pleased if she wist how men do worship unto her on the

earth. And the like, I trow, may be said of all
God's saints."

At the conclusion of his sermon, Sastre leaned
forward over the pulpit and spoke in a low, earnest,
loving tone. " Who is here, good friends," asked he,
" that loveth this blessed Lord Jesu, the Lamb that
was slain ? Who is here who will give up this vile
and wretched world for His sake ? Who that will
sue[1] this blessed Lamb whithersoever He goeth,
even though He lead along the sharp way called
tribulation, or the weary way called prison, or the
bitter way called poverty, or even verily through
the low and dark door called death ? Who is here ?
Is there none I beseech you, good friends, hath Christ
no souls in this place ? When the blessed angels
count up the number of the purchased ones, will
ye have them leave Bostock out of their reckoning ?
Shall it be worse than Sodom and Gomorrah, wherein
there was *one* soul that was saved ? Is there not *one*
here ? Nay, brethren, I trust it is not so. I trust ye
will come, yea in numbers, yea in throngs, yea in
multitudes, and crowd on Christ to touch the hem of
His blessed garment, that is the power of His great
mercy. Christ loveth to have folk crowd on Him to

[1] Follow.

cry Him mercy. I read not that ever He complained of the crowding of the multitude. I read not that ever He turned away so much as one poor caitiff[1] sinner who came unto Him. I read not that His lips plained ever of aught but that they came not—that they lacked faith. I am an old man, friends, and in all likelihood shall I never come here again; but I say unto you that I shall scan well the multitude in the white apparel for the faces which be upturned unto me this day. I pray you that I miss them not. I pray God that ye—yea, that every man and woman of you, may be clothed in yon glistering and shene[2] raiment, and may lift up your voices to cry, 'The Lamb is worthy' in the city of God!"

That sermon was a strange thing to Margery Lovell. Never, from the day of her birth to that day, had she heard as she now heard of the Lamb that was slain. For above a mile of their way home Richard and Margery kept perfect silence, which the latter was the first to break just before they came in sight of Lovell Tower.

"Master Pynson, we have heard strange things to-day."

"We have, of a truth, Mistress Margery. I wonder whether Master Sastre be right."

---

[1] Miserable   [2] Bright.

"I wish greatly," replied Margery, "that I could get the book wherein I have heard that Master Wycliffe rendered God's Word into the vulgar tongue. I could see then whether Master Sastre were right. I would I knew of any man who had that book!"

"Master Carew of Marston told me some time agone," said Richard, rather hesitatingly, "that he had the Gospel according to John the Apostle, copied out by a feat[1] scribe from Master Wycliffe's rendering thereof."

"O Master Pynson!" said Margery, entreatingly, "I pray you that you ask good Master Carew to lend me that book! Tell him that Mistress Margery Lovell will lay her best jewels to pledge that she returneth the book safe. I must see that book Master Pynson!"

"Softly, I pray you, good Mistress Margery," answered Richard, smiling; "it were well to go warily to work; for wot you not that Master Wycliffe —ay, and Master Sastre too—be accounted heretics by some? You would not, trow, fall under the ban of Holy Church?"

"I would with a good will do aught, or bear aught," replied Margery, earnestly, "so I might wit of a surety that I should be one of those who wear the

---

[1] Clever.

white apparel, and cry, 'The Lamb is worthy' in the city of God!'"

"Well, Mistress Margery," said Richard, soothingly, "I will do my best for to get you the book, but it may be some time ere I see Master Carew."

Dame Lovell herself was standing on the steps of Lovell Tower, apparently looking out for the riders, for as soon as they came within hearing distance she raised her voice to say, "Richard Pynson! Sir Geoffrey would speak with you. Come in quickly, I pray you, and leave the handmaidens to help Mistress Margery from her pillion."

"I need no help, good mother," said Margery, as she sprang lightly from her seat, while Richard hurried into the house to find Sir Geoffrey.

"Sir Geoffrey would send Richard Pynson to Marston," said Dame Lovell, as she preceded Margery into the hall. "And how liked you Master Sastre, Madge?"

"Very greatly, good mother; never heard I before a homily so brave."

"That is well," said Dame Lovell, and disappeared into the kitchen, as Margery ran up-stairs to her own room, and brought down in her hand a valuable necklace. Richard came into the banqueting-hall from one door, as Margery made her appearance from the opposite one.

"I have a letter from Sir Geoffrey to bear to Sir Ralph Marston," said he. "Have you any commands for Marston, Mistress Margery?" he mischievously added.

"Master Pynson," said Margery, earnestly, in a low tone, "I pray you to take this jewel to Master Carew, and to leave it in pledge with him, in case he will lend me the book. If he value it at more than this, I can send other jewels; but, Master Pynson, bring me the book!"

Richard placed the necklace for safety in the bosom of his doublet, and answered, "Fear not, good mistress; if I bring you not the book, it shall not be for lack of entreaty. Only hope not too much, for I may chance to fail."

"Pray God he lend you the book!" was her only answer.

CHAPTER II.

A LATE DINNER.

"And there is something in this book
That makes all care be gone,
And yet I weep—I know not why—
As I go reading on!"
—MARY HOWITT.

MARGERY went into the kitchen, and helped to prepare supper, under the directions of Dame Lovell, and then she returned to her own room, and tried to finish her illumination of Peter and Malchus; but she could not command her thoughts sufficiently to paint well, so much was her heart set on "the book." Therefore she sat with her hands folded in her lap, and tried to recall Sastre's sermon. Then came supper-time, and Margery went down to the banqueting-hall; and after supper, having begged her parents' blessing before retiring to rest, she came back to her chamber. But she did not attempt to undress. When the sun set, a red glory above the tree-tops, she was watching at her casement for Richard Pynson; and when the silver moon and

the little golden stars had taken the sun's place in the
heavens, she was watching still. At last she heard
the sound of a horse's feet, and stole softly down the
private staircase which led from her room to the
hall. As Richard entered the hall, Margery softly
murmured his name.

"What, Mistress Margery!" he cried, in astonishment. "You here! You have watched well for
the book, and—there it is."

And Richard drew from the bag slung over his
shoulder a small quarto volume.

"Oh, thanks, good Master Pynson, a thousand
thanks!" cried Margery, in delight. "And how long
season may I keep the book?"

"Master Carew said," returned Pynson, "that he
asked not jewels for the safe-keeping of the book,
for the word of a Lovell was enough," and Richard
drew the necklace from his bosom and handed it to
Margery. "He will lend the book for one month's
time. He said, furthermore, that he lent it, not
because he loved it not, but because he prayed that
you, Mistress Margery, might know and love it
too."

"Amen!" was Margery's answer, as she folded
the book to her bosom, and crept softly back to her

chamber—but not to bed. The first thing she did was to take off her petticoat and cote-hardie, and to put on a loose dressing-gown of gray serge. Then she divested herself of her head-dress, and allowed her fair hair to flow down over her shoulders without restraint. Having thus rendered herself comfortable, she seated herself in a carved chair, furnished with an ample cushion, and proceeded to examine the book.

The book was bound in leather, dark brown in colour, and simple in workmanship. It was clasped with two small clasps of common metal, washed over with silver; the leaves were of vellum, and on the first page was a badly-drawn and violently-coloured illumination of Christ and the Samaritan woman. Stops (as a rule) it had not, except a full stop here and there; and capitals there were none, with the occasional exception of a letter in red ink. Notwithstanding this, the manuscript, being written in a clear small hand, was very legible to eyes accustomed to read only black letter. At first Margery felt as if she were doing wrong in reading the book, but her curiosity drew her on, as well as her earnest desire to know more of those " strange things " of which Sastre had spoken in his sermon. Margery had taken the precaution of fastening the door before she commenced the study of the book. After the first glance which had made her acquainted with the particulars above noticed, she opened the book at random near the middle, and her eye fell on the following words :—

"*Be not your herte afrayed, ne drede it ; ye bileuen in God, and bileeue ye in me. In the hous of my Fadir ben manye dwellingis ; if ony thinge lasse, I hadde seid to you ; for I go to make readi to you a place. And if I go to make redy to you a place, eftsoone I come, and I schal take you to my silf, that where I am, ye be.*"[1]

Never before had Margery read words like these. "Be not your herte afrayed !" Why, the one feeling which she was taught was more acceptable to God than any other, was fear. "In the hous of my Fadir ben manye dwellingis." Margery clasped her hands above her head, and laid head and hands upon the open volume ; and in the agony of her earnestness she cried aloud, "O Lamb that was slain, hast thou not made ready a dwelling for Margery Lovell ! "

Margery read on, and the more she read the more she wondered. The Church did not teach as this book did, and *both* could not be right. Which, then, was wrong ? How could the Church be wrong, which was the depository of God's truth ? And yet, how

[1] John xiv. 1-3.

could the holy apostle be wrong in reporting the words of Christ ?

Many times over during that night did Margery's thoughts arrange themselves in this manner. At one time she thought that nothing could possibly supersede the infallibility of the Church ; at another she saw the complete impossibility of anything being able to stand for a moment against the infallibility of God. The only conclusion at which she could arrive was a determination to read the volume, and judge for herself. She read on. *" I am weye, treuthe, and lyf ; no man cometh to the Fadir but by me."* [1] Were these words the words of Christ ? And what way had Margery been taught ? Obedience to the Church, humility, penances, alms-giving—works always, Christ never. Could these be the right way ? She went on, till the tears ran down her cheeks like rain—till her heart throbbed and her soul glowed with feelings she had never felt before—till the world, and life, and death, and things present, all seemed to be nothing, and Christ alone seemed to be everything. She read on, utterly oblivious of the flight of time, and regardless that darkness had given place to light, until the fall of something in the room below, and the voice

---

[1] John xiv. 6.

of Dame Lovell calling for Cicely, suddenly warned
her that the house was astir. Margery sprang up,
her heart beating now for a different reason. She
hurriedly closed the book, and secreted it in a private
cupboard, of which she alone had the key, and where
she generally kept her jewels, and any little trinkets
on which she set a special value. Margery's next
act, I fear, was indefensible ; for it was to throw the
cover and pillows of her bed into confusion, that the
maids might suppose it had been occupied as usual.
She then noiselessly unfastened the door, and proceeded with her dressing, so that when, a few minutes
after, Dame Lovell came panting up the stairs, and
lifted the latch, the only thing she noticed was Margery
standing before the mirror, and fastening up her hair
with what she called a pin, and what we should, I
suspect, designate a metallic skewer.

" What, Madge, not donned yet ? " was Dame
Lovell's greeting. " How thou hast overslept thyself,
girl ! Dost know it is already five of the clock, and
thy father and I have been stirring above an hour ? "

" Is it so late, of a truth ? " asked Margery, in
dismay. " I cry you mercy, good mother ! "

And Margery was thinking what excuse she could
use by way of apology, when Dame Lovell's next

words set her at rest, as they showed that the mind of that good lady was full of other thoughts than her daughter's late rising.

"Grand doings, lass!" said she, as she sat down in the carved arm-chair. "Grand doings, of a truth, Madge!"

"Where, good mistress mine?"

"Where?" said Dame Lovell, lifting her eyebrows. "Why, here, in Lovell Tower. Where should they be else? Richard Pynson was so late of returning from Marston that he saw not thy father until this morrow."

"I heard him come."

"Wert awake?"

"Yea. I was awake a long season!"

"Poor lass!" said her mother. "No marvel thou art late. But harken to what I was about to tell thee. Sir Ralph Marston and his kinsman the Lord Marnell, dine with us to-day."

"To-day?"

"Yea, to-day. Dear, dear, dear, dear! What folk must they be that live in London town! Marry, Sir Ralph sent word by Richard Pynson, praying us not to dine until one of the clock, for that the Lord Marnell is not used to it at an earlier hour. I marvel when they sup! I trow it is not until all Christian folk be a-bed!"

"Dwells the Lord Marnell in London?" inquired Margery, with surprise; for Margery was more astonished and interested to hear of a nobleman from London dining with her parents than a modern young lady would be if told that a Chinese mandarin was expected.

"Yea, truly, in London dwells he, and is of the bedchamber to our Lord the King, and a great man, Madge! Hie thee down when thou art dressed, child, and make up thy choicest dishes. But, good Saint Christopher! how shall I do from seven to one of the clock without eating? I will bid Cicely serve a void at ten."

And so saying, Dame Lovell bustled downstairs as quickly as her corpulence would allow her, and Margery followed, a few minutes later. While the former was busy in the hall, ordering fresh rushes to be spread, and the tables set, Margery repaired to the ample kitchen, where, summoning the maids to assist her, and tying a large coarse apron round her, she proceeded to concoct various dishes, reckoned at that time particularly choice. There are few books more curious than a cookery-book five hundred years old.

Our forefathers appear to have used joints of meat much less frequently than the smaller creatures, whether flesh or fowl, hares, rabbits, chickens, capons, &c. Of fish, eels excepted, they ate little or none out of Lent. Potatoes, of course, they had none; and rice was so rare that it figured as a "spice;" but to make up for this, they ate, apparently, almost every green thing that grew in their gardens, rose-leaves not excepted. Of salt they had an unutterable abhorrence. Sugar existed, but it was very expensive, and honey was often used instead. Pepper and cloves were employed in immense quantities. The article which appears to have held with them the corresponding place to that of salt with us, and which was never omitted in any dish, no matter what its other component parts, was saffron. In corroboration of these remarks, I append one very curious receipt,— a dish which formed one of the principal covers on Sir Geoffrey Lovell's table :—

" FARSURE OF HARE.

" Take hares and flee [flay] hom, and washe hom in broth of fleshe with the blode; then boyle the brothe and scome [skim] hit wel and do hit in a pot, and more brothe thereto. And take onyons and mynce hom and put hom in the pot, and set hit on the fyre and let hit sethe, [boil ;] and take bred and stepe hit in wyn and vynegur, and drawe hit up and do hit in the potte, and pouder of pepur and clowes, and maces hole, [whole,] and pynes, and raysynges of corance, [currants ;] then take and parboyle wel the hare, and choppe hym on gobettes [small pieces] and put him into a faire [clean] urthen pot ; and do thereto clene grese, and set hit on the fyre, and stere hit wele tyl hit be wel fryed ; then caste hit in the pot to the broth, an do therto pouder of canell [cinnamon] and sugur ; and let hit boyle togedur, and colour hit wyth saffron, and serve hit forthe."

It will be noticed from this that our ancestors had none of our vulgar prejudices with respect to onions, neither had they any regard to the Scriptural prohibition of blood. The utter absence of all prescription of quantities in these receipts is delightfully indefinite.

There were many other dishes to this important dinner beside the " farsure of hare ; " and on this occasion most of the rabbits and chickens were entire, and not " chopped on gobbettes ; " for the feast was " for a lord," and lords were permitted to eat whole birds and beasts, while the less privileged commonalty had to content themselves with "gob-bettes."

When Margery had concluded her preparations for dinner, she went into the garden to gather rosemary and flowers, which she disposed in various parts of the hall, laying large bunches of rosemary in all available places. All was now ready, and Margery washed her hands, took off her apron, and ran up into her own room, to pin on her shoulder a "quintise," in other words, a long streamer of cherry-coloured ribbon.

The guests arrived on horseback about half-past twelve, and Richard Pynson ushered them into the hall, and ran into the kitchen to inform Dame Lovell and Margery, adding that "he pitied Lord Marnell's horse," a remark the signification of which became apparent when the ladies presented themselves in the banqueting-hall. Sir Geoffrey was already there, conversing with his guests. Margery expected to find Lord Marnell similar to his cousin, Sir Ralph Marston, whom she already knew, and who was a pleasant, gentlemanly man of about forty years of age, always joking with everybody, and full of fun. But she did not expect what she now saw.

The great man from London, who sat in a large

oak-chair in the hall, was a great man in all corporeal senses. He was very tall, and stout in proportion ; an older man than his cousin. Sir Ralph, perhaps ten or fifteen years older ; and there was something in his face which made Margery drop her eyes in an instant. It was a very curious face. The upper part —the eyes and forehead—was finely formed, and showed at least an average amount of intellect ; but from the nose downward the form and expression of the features were suggestive only of the animal,— a brutal, sensual, repelling look. Margery, who had looked for the great man from London with girlish curiosity, suddenly felt an unconquerable and causeless dislike to him swell up in her heart, a something which she could neither define nor account for, that made her wish to avoid sitting near him, and turn her eyes away whenever his were directed towards her.

Sir Geoffrey presented his wife and daughter to Lord Marnell, and Sir Ralph came forward with a cordial greeting ; after which they took their seats at table, for Richard Pynson was already bringing in the "farsure of hare," and Mistress Katherine following with the pottage. The occupants of the high table, on the daïs, consisted of Sir Geoffrey and

Dame Lovell, Lord Marnell, Sir Ralph Marston, Margery, Richard Pynson, Mistress Katherine, and Friar Andrew Rous, Sir Geoffrey's chaplain. The maids sat at the second table, and the farm-servants at a third, lower down the hall. Sir Ralph, as usual, was full of fun, and spared nobody, keeping the whole table in a roar of laughter, excepting Lord Marnell, who neither laughed at his cousin's jokes, nor offered any observations of his own, being wholly occupied with the discussion of the various dishes as they were presented to him, and consuming, according to the joint testimony of Dame Lovell and Friar Andrew after the feast, "enough to last seven men for a week." When dinner was over, and "the tables lifted," the company gathered round the fire, and proceeded to make themselves comfortable. Sir Ralph sang songs, and told funny anecdotes, and cracked jokes with the young people; while Lord Marnell, in conversation with Sir Geoffrey, showed that the promise of neither half of his face was entirely unfulfilled, by proving himself a shrewd observer, and not a bad talker. In the midst of this conversation, Sir Ralph, turning round to Sir Geoffrey, inquired if he had heard anything of a certain sermon that had been preached the day before at Bostock Church.

"I heard of it," answered he, "but I heard it not. Some of mine, methinks, heard the same. Madge, wentest not thou thereto?"

"Ay, good father, I went with Master Pynson."

"Ah!" said Sir Ralph. "I went not, for the which I now grieve, the more as my good cousin telleth me that Master Sastre is accounted a great one by some—but these seem not of the best."

"Misconceive me not, fair cousin," said Lord Marnell. "It is only the Lollards that think well of the man, and thou wottest that Holy Church looketh not kindly on their evil doings. That ill priest, John Wycliffe, who is accounted their leader, hath done more hurt to the faith than any heretic these many years."

"Thou art but ill affected unto them, I trow," said Sir Ralph, jokingly.

"Ill affected!" exclaimed Lord Marnell, bringing down his hand violently upon the arm of his chair, with a blow which made Margery start. "I cry you mercy, fair mistress—but if I knew of any among my kin or meynie[1] that leaned that way—ay, were it mine own sister, the Prioress of Kennington—I

[1] Household retinue.

tell thee, Ralph, I would have her up before the King's Grace's council, and well whipped!"

Margery shuddered slightly. Sir Ralph leaned back in his chair, and laughed heartily.

"Well said, fair cousin mine! But I pray thee, tell me what doctrines hold these men, that thou wouldst have them all up afore the King's Grace's council, and well whipped?"

"All manner of evil!" answered Lord Marnell, wrathfully. "They hold, as I hear, that the blessed Sacrament of the Altar is in no wise the true body of Christ, but only a piece of bread blessed by the priest, and to be eaten in memory of His death; for the which reason also they would allow the lay folk to drink Christ's blood. Moreover, they say that the blessed angels and God's saints be not to be worshipped, but only to be held in reverence and kindly memory. Also, they give to the common people the Scriptures of God's Word for to read, which we wot well is only fit for priests. And in all things which they do, I find not that these evil wretches do hold any true thing as taught by Holy Church, but one, which is masses for souls departed. I wis not much concerning them, for they move mine anger."

"I pray your good Lordship," asked Sir Geoffrey,

"can you tell me whether these men be in great force in London or thereabouts at this time? Find they any favour in the Court?"

"They be ever increasing," said Lord Marnell, "so much so that the King's council have seen good to prepare some orders against them—forbidding of their assemblages, and such like—for to present unto the Parliament. These orders provide, as my good friend holy Abbot Bilson did tell me, that all convicted to be Lollards shall suffer close prison, for longer or shorter time, as pleaseth the King's Grace. I trow they find not favour at Court with many, but the few that look well on them be unhaply of the highest. I have heard say that some in the Duke of Lancaster's palace show them favour, and it is no news that the Queen—whose soul God pardon!—did lean that way. In all open hours she was reading of Scripture in the vulgar tongue. Master Sastre, the priest, who my fair cousin telleth me was a-preaching in Bostock Church yestermorn, is, I take it, one of their chief men, and did learn of Master Wycliffe himself. I trow he will find it go hard with him if ever he cometh near London again. He goeth a-preaching of his doctrines up and down the realm, and perverting from the faith evilly-disposed men and sely[1] damsels who lack something to set their tongues running."

Sir Ralph here made a remark which turned the conversation; for this Margery was sorry, as it had interested her extremely. Lord Marnell's remarks taught her more about the Lollards than she had ever known before. So the Queen read the Bible in English! thought she. Why should not I do the same? She sat wrapped in her own thoughts for a long time, and when she roused herself from them, she noticed that Dame Lovell had quitted the room, and that Sir Ralph and Sir Geoffrey were talking politics, wherein they were occupied in proving, to the unqualified satisfaction of each, that there was "something rotten in the State," and that England could not last very long, her only business being to demolish France. And Margery, finding the conversation now extremely dull—though had she for an instant suspected the turn it would take in her absence, she certainly would never have gone—slipped out, and joined the more noisy party in the kitchen, where she found Dame Lovell seated in the chimney-corner and inveighing fervently against late hours.

"An it be not three of the clock already," said

[1] Simple, unlearned.

that angry lady, "I am a heathen Jew, and no Christian! Time to prepare supper for Christian folk—but when that great hulk of a man, that can do nothing in this world but eat, thinks to sup, I wis not! Marry, I trow that nought more will go down his throat until evensong! I marvel if our grandsons will be as great fools as we be!"

"More, Dame," answered Mistress Katherine, sententiously. She was a woman who very seldom spoke, and when she did, compressed all her ideas into as few words as would serve the purpose.

"Nay, Saint Christopher! I hope not," said Dame Lovell. "And what am I for to do now? Madge, lass, open the door and bid hither Richard Pynson."

Margery softly opened the door into the hall; and as softly called the person who answered to that name. He rose, and came to her, and Sir Geoffrey and Lord Marnell, who were in low-toned, earnest conversation, suddenly stopped as she appeared.

"Richard," said Dame Lovell, in what she doubtlessly intended for a whisper, "I pray thee, good youth, to go in softly, and privily demand of Sir Ralph what time he list to sup."

Richard executed the order, and, returning, closed the door behind him.

"Sir Ralph saith, good mistress mine, that the Lord Marnell when at home suppeth not afore six of the clock; but he prayeth you for to sup when you will, to the which he will without doubt accommodate himself."

"Six of the clock!" cried Dame Lovell, in amazement. Richard, art sure thou heardest aright?"

"Certes, good mistress."

Dame Lovell sat in silent horror.

"Well!" said she at length, "if ever in all my days did I hear of a like thing! Cicely, serve a void in my privy chamber at four of the clock. This poor country of ours may well go to wrack, if its rulers sup not afore six of the clock! Dear, dear, dear! I marvel if the blessed Virgin Saint Mary supped not until six of the clock! May all the saints forgive us that we be such fools!"

CHAPTER III.

COMING EVENTS CAST THEIR SHADOWS BEFORE.

" Ay, sooth we feel too strong in weal to need Thee on that road,
But woe being come, the soul is dumb that crieth not on God."
—ELIZABETH BARRETT BROWNING.

THE guests departed about seven o'clock, and Dame Lovell got to bed a little before nine —an hour which was in her eyes most untimely. Margery, though she had not slept on the previous night, was unable to close her eyes for some time. The unwonted excitement kept her awake, and another idea, too, mingled with her thoughts. The book! How should she copy it ? It must be at stolen hours —probably in the night. And what material should she use ? Not vellum, for Sir Geoffrey might ask what she was doing if she requested more of that precious article than was necessary for her Breviary. He had allowed her some paper for the rough draft of her illuminations, and she had a little of this left. She determined to make use of this paper so far as it would go, and to trust to circumstances for the remainder.

Thinking and contriving, Margery sank to sleep, and dreamed that Sir Geoffrey was reading the book to Lord Marnell, who, by that curious mixture which often takes place in dreams, was also Richard Pynson. From this dream, about ten minutes after she fell asleep, as it appeared to her, Margery suddenly sprang up to the conviction that broad daylight was streaming in at the window. She rose and dressed herself hurriedly, and, running down into the kitchen, was surprised to find nobody there but Joan, the drudge of the household, who moreover was rubbing her eyes, and apparently only half awake.

" Why, Mistress Margery ! " said the girl, in astonishment, " your good mistress-ship is early, considering our late hours. The Dame is not yet risen."

" In good sooth ? " inquired Margery, looking at the clock, when she found to her surprise that it was barely five o'clock ; and receiving from Joan the information that Dame Lovell had told Cicely overnight that she did not intend to appear until six, she returned to her own room, and, drawing the book from its hiding-place, commenced her task of copying. Margery worked quickly, and had copied nearly a page in the hour. So absorbed was she in her task, that she never heard the door open, and started like a guilty thing when the well-known voice of her mother sounded close by her.

"Eh, Madge! Up and at work? Thou wilt work thy fingers to the bone, child! Is that thy mass-book? Nay, it is paper, I see, and that, I wis, is on vellum. What art doing, damsel?"

Pale and red, red and pale, went Margery by turns at this string of questions.

"Why, lass, what hast?" asked Dame Lovell, in surprise.

"I cry you mercy, good mother!" said Margery, descending to equivocation, and blushing more than ever; "I heard you not open my door, and your voice started me."

"Poor Madge! did I fright thee?" said Dame Lovell, kindly. "But what is this, child? Another Breviary? Dost want two?"

"Poor Madge" she was indeed at this moment. Terrified beyond measure lest Dame Lovell should inform Sir Geoffrey, whose learned eyes would perceive in a moment what the book was—and seeing more danger in his discovering its real character than in letting him suppose it to be another Breviary,

Margery, generally so truth-telling, was frightened into a lie.

"Ay, good mother," she stammered out, "'tis a Breviary."

All that day Margery sat upon thorns; but Dame Lovell made no mention of the incident, and she accordingly hoped it was forgotten.

Day after day passed on, and Margery worked harder than ever at copying the book. She finished her task just one day before the month was up, and gave back the original to Richard Pynson, entreating him to make an errand to Marston as soon as possible, and restore the book, with her hearty thanks, into the hands of Master Carew.

On the evening of that day, Dame Lovell sat at work in the wide chimney-corner of the hall. Near her was Mistress Katherine, scraping almonds into a bowl; while Margery, occupied with her distaff, sat at a little distance. On a wide oaken settle on the opposite side of the fire lay Friar Andrew, taking a nap, as was his afternoon custom; while on another settle drawn up before the fire, Sir Geoffrey and Richard Pynson sat conversing with the ladies.

"Madge, lass, hast finished thy Breviary?" asked Sir Geoffrey. "An thou hast, I would see it."

Margery's heart leaped into her mouth, for now was the time for the discovery of her falsehood to be made. Simply replying, however, " I will seek it, father," she rose and laid her distaff down.

" Ay, Madge is a feat scribe, truly ! " remarked Dame Lovell, to Margery's unspeakable distress. " She hath written two Breviaries, I wis."

" Two ! " said Sir Geoffrey, laughing. " One for Sundays and feasts, and the other for week-days ? Madge, bring us both of them."

Margery left the room, and returned in a few minutes, with both the books in her hand. Sir Geoffrey took them, and opened the illuminated one—the genuine Breviary—first. Margery reseated herself, and took up her distaff, but the thread was very uneven, and she broke it twice, while her father turned over the leaves of the book, and praised her writing and illuminations. His praise was sweet enough, but some time he must come to the end, and *then*——! How fervently Margery wished that Dame Lovell would ask an irrelevant question, which might lead to conversation—that Friar Andrew would awake— that Cicely would rush in with news of the cows having broken into the garden—or that *anything* would occur which would put a stop to the examination of those volumes before Sir Geoffrey arrived at the last leaf! But everything, as it always is under such circumstances, was unusually quiet; and Sir Geoffrey fastened the silver clasps of the Breviary, and opened the book without anything to hinder his doing so. Margery stole furtive looks at her father over her distaff, and soon observed an ominous look of displeasure creeping over his face. He passed over several leaves—turned to the beginning, and then to the end,—then, closing the volume, he looked up and said, in a stern voice—

" Andrew ! "

Friar Andrew snored placidly on.

" Andrew ! " said Sir Geoffrey, in a louder tone.

Friar Andrew gave an indistinct sound between a snore and a grunt. Sir Geoffrey rose from his seat, and striding over to where his confessor slept, laid hold of his shoulders, and gave him such a shake as nearly brought him to the stone floor.

" Awake, thou sluggard ! " said he, angrily. " Is it a time for the shepherd to sleep when the wolf is already in the fold, and the lambs be in danger ? "

" Eh ? Oh ! ay ! " said Friar Andrew, half awake. " Time to sup, eh ? "

" Look here, Andrew ! " roared his offended patron,

" and see thee what this sinful maid hath been doing. What penance deemest thou fit for such fault as this ? "

He handed the book to the friar. The friar sat up, rubbed his eyes, opened the book, and turned over two or three leaves.

" I cry your good worship mercy," said he. " I knew not you were assaying to arouse me. I was dreaming of a kettle of furmety of Madge's making."

" I trow here is a pretty kettle of furmety of Madge's making ! " was the irate response.

" I conceive you not, good master," said the friar. " The book is a good book enough, trow."

" Thou art an ass ! " was the civil answer. " Seest thou not that it is the translation of Scripture whereof the Lord Marnell spake, by Master John Wycliffe, the Lollard priest ? Mindest thou not that which he said about Lollards ? "

" An what if it be ? " said the confessor, yawning. " I pin not my faith on my Lord Marnell's sleeve, though it *were* made of slashed velvet. And I trow Madge hath been too well bred up to draw evil from the book. So let the damsel alone, good master, and give her book back. I trow it will never harm her."

Margery was exceedingly surprised at the turn

which affairs were taking. The truth was, that Friar Andrew was very fond of her; he had been Sir Geoffrey's chaplain before she was born, she had grown up under his eye, and she made, moreover, such a kettle of furmety as he declared no one else could make. Beside this, Andrew was a marvellous poor scholar; he could never read a book at sight, and required to spell it over two or three times before he could make out the meaning. He could read his mass-book, because he had done so for the last forty years, and could have gone through the service as easily without book as with it; though, had a different copy been given him, in which the pages did not commence with the same line, it would probably have perplexed him extremely. Thus, under these circumstances, his love for Margery, his love for furmety, and his utter ignorance, combined to dispose him to let her off easily.

Sir Geoffrey took the book from his chaplain with a sort of growl, and threw it into Margery's lap.

"There! take it, damsel!" said he. "I account it Andrew's business to take care of thy soul, and he saith it will not hurt thee. I mind it the less, as thou wilt shortly go to dwell with one who will see to thee in these matters, and will not let thee read Lollard books."

The thread fell from Margery's hand, and so did the distaff, which rolled over the floor with a clatter. She never heeded it. A terrible, indefinite dread had taken hold of her.

"Father! what mean you?" she stammered forth at last.

"What mean I?" said Sir Geoffrey, in the same half-affectionate, half-sarcastic tone. "Why, that I have promised thee to the Lord Marnell, Lord of the Bedchamber to the King's Grace, and Knight of the Garter—and thou wilt be a lady and dwell in London town, and hold up thine head with the highest! What sayest to *that*, child?" he added, proudly.

She sat a moment with her white lips parted,— cold, silent, stunned. Then the bitter cry of "Father, father!" awoke the echoes of the old hall.

Sir Geoffrey was evidently troubled. He had sought only his daughter's grandeur, and had never so much as dreamed that he might be making her miserable.

"Why, child! dost not like it?" said he, in surprise.

She rose from her seat, and went to him, and kneeling down by him, laid her head, bowed on her clasped hands, upon his knee. "O father, father!" was all she said again.

"Truly, lass, I grieve much to see thee thus," said her father, in a perplexed tone. "But thou wilt soon get over this, and be right glad, too, to be so grand a lady. What shall I say to comfort thee?"

Long, terrible, hysterical sobs were coming from the bowed frame—but no tears. At length, still without lifting up her head, she whispered—

"Is there no way to shun it, father? I love him not. O father, I love him not—I cannot love him!"

"Truly, my poor lass, I trow we cannot shun it," said he. "I never thought to see thee grieve so sore. The Lord Marnell is a noble gentleman, and will find thee in silken tissues and golden cauls."

Sir Geoffrey did not rightly understand his daughter's sorrow. His "silken tissues and golden cauls" did not raise the bowed head one inch.

"Father!" she whispered, "have you promised him?"

"I have, my child," he answered, softly.

She rose suddenly, and quickly turned to go up the stairs leading to her own room. At this moment Richard Pynson rose also, and quietly taking up the book, which had fallen from Margery's lap on the floor, he handed it to her. She took it with one hand, and gave him the other, but did not let him see her face. Then she passed into her chamber, and they heard her fasten the door.

When she had done so, she flung herself down on the rushes,[1] and bent her head forward on her knees. The longer she thought over her prospects, the more dreary and doleful they appeared. Her state of mind was one that has been touchingly described by a writer who lived three hundred years later—" Sidney's sister, Pembroke's mother "—who, of all who have attempted and failed in the impossible task of rendering the Psalms into verse, perhaps approached as near success as any one.

> " Troublous seas doe mee surrownde ;
> Saue, O LORD, my sinking soule,
> Sinking wheare it feeles no grownde,
> In this gulf, this whirling hole ;
> Wayghting ayde with earnest eying,
> Calling God with bootles crying ;
> Dymme and drye in mee are fownde
> Eyes to see, and throate to sounde."

Suddenly, as she sat thus bowed down, too sorrowful

[1] Carpets were very rare at this time, and only used on state occasions and for invalids. Their place was supplied by fresh green rushes, strewn on the floor. It appears rather doubtful, however, whether carpets were not sometimes used in the winter.

for tears, like the dew to a parched flower came the words of the book—nay, the words of the Lord—into her soul.

"*Be not your herte afrayed, ne drede it.*" "*And therfore ghe han now sorowe, but eftsoone I schal se ghou, and ghoure herte schal haue ioie, and no man schal take fro ghou ghoure ioie. Treuly, treuly, I seie to ghou, if ghe axen the Fadir ony thing in my name he schal ghyue to ghou.*"[1]

Now, Margery had neither teacher nor commentary to interpret to her the words of Scripture; and the result was, that she never dreamed of modifying any of them, but took the words simply and literally. It never entered her head to interpret them with any qualification—to argue that "anything" must mean only some things. Ah! how much better would it be for us, if we would accept those blessed words as plainly, as unconditionally, as conclusively, as this poor untaught girl!

But when Margery considered the question more minutely, poor child! she knew not what to ask. The constant reference of everything by the Lord Jesus to "the will of the Father" had struck her forcibly; and now she dared not ask for entire freedom

[1] John xvi. 22, 23.

from the crushing blow which had fallen on her, lest it should not be the will of the Father. So she contented herself with a supplication which, under the circumstances, was the best she could have offered. She did not even try to form her petitions into words —the depths in which her soul lay were too deep for that ; it was a wordless cry which went up to God. But its substance was an entreaty that the Father would do His will, and would bend her will to it ; that whatever He saw fit to give her, He would always give His presence and His love ; that whatever He was pleased to take away, He would not take from her the word unto His handmaid wherein He had caused her to hope. And when she rose from her knees, the prominent idea in her mind might have been expressed in the words of the old proverb, " He loseth nothing that keepeth God for his friend."

An hour afterwards, Dame Lovell, who could not rest for the remembrance of her child's grief, came softly into Margery's chamber to see if she could comfort her. She was surprised to find her sleeping as quietly as a little child, with the book, even in sleep, held fast to her bosom, as if she would permit nothing to separate her from that Word of God which had given rest to her soul.

CHAPTER IV.

LIFE IN LONDON.

"Whan we cam' in by Glasgow toun,
We were a comely sicht to see,—
My luve was clad in velvet black
And I mysel' in cramoisie."
—OLD BALLAD.

A FORTNIGHT after the events recorded in the last chapter, Lovell Tower was in the confusion of great preparations for the approaching wedding. Friar Andrew was despatched to York fair to purchase twenty yards of scarlet cloth, fourteen yards of tawny satin, eight of purple satin, and the same number of blue cloth of silver, with jewels and rich furs. All was cutting-out and fitting-on, with discussions about trimmings, quintises, and head-dresses. Richard Pynson was sent hither and thither on errands. Sir Geoffrey himself superintended the purchase of a new pillion, and ordered it to be covered with green velvet. Lord Marnell, who did not often come to Lovell Tower himself, sent over a trusty messenger every day to inquire if Mistress Margery had rested well and was merry. From the latter condition she was very far. At length the preparations were completed; and on a splendid summer day, when the birds were singing their most joyous melodies, Margery Lovell was married, in Bostock Church, to Sir Ralph Marnell, Baron Marnell of Lymington, Knight of the Garter. The bride was attired in blue cloth of silver, trimmed with miniver; and her hair, as was then the custom at weddings, was not confined by any head-dress, but flowed down her back, long and straight. The bridegroom was dressed in cramoisie—crimson velvet—richly trimmed with bullion, and wore three long waving plumes in his cap, as well as a streamer of gold lace. If any one who may read these pages should inquire why Margery chose blue for her wedding-dress, I may answer that Margery would have been greatly astonished if any one had recommended white. White at this period was not only a mourning colour, but mourning of the very deepest character.

No pains were spared to make this a merry wedding, and yet it certainly could not be called a joyous one. All the inhabitants of Lovell Tower knew well that the bride was very far from happy; Sir Geoffrey and

Dame Lovell were naturally sorry to lose their only child ; Friar Andrew mourned over his favourite and his kettle of furmety ; while Richard Pynson had his own private sorrow, to which I need not allude further in this place.

The bridal feast was held at Lovell Tower, and all the neighbours were invited to it. The festivities were prolonged to a late hour ; and at five o'clock next morning everybody was busy helping the bride to pack up. Everybody thought of everything so well, that there was very little left for her to think of ; but she did think of one thing. When Margery set out for her new home in London, the book went too.

The journey to London from the North was in those days a long and wearisome one. There were no vehicles but litters and waggons. Margery travelled part of the way in a litter, and part on a pillion behind her bridegroom, who rode on horseback the whole way. He had with him a regular army of retainers, besides sundry maidens for the Lady Marnell, at the head of whom was Alice Jordan, the unlucky girl who, at our first visit to Lovell Tower, was reprimanded for leaving out the onions in the blanch-porre. Margery had persuaded her mother to resign to her

E

for a personal attendant this often clumsy and forgetful but really well-meaning girl. It was a Friday evening when they arrived in London; and Margery was much too tired to think of doing anything but rest her wearied head in sleep.

As early as four o'clock the next morning, she was roused by London cries from a happy dream of Lovell Tower. "Quinces! sweet quinces! ripe quinces!" "Any kitchen-stuff, have you, maids?" "Cakes and ale! cakes and ale!" "Cherry ripe! cherry ripe!" "Come buy, pretty maids, come buy! come buy!" with an undercurrent of the long rhymed cry of the hawker of haberdashery, of which Shakespeare has given us a specimen as regards the English version—

"Lawn, as white as driven snow;
Cyprus, black as e'er was crow," &c.

Margery lay still, and listened in silence to all these new sounds. At length she rose and dressed herself, with the assistance of Alice, who was seriously dissatisfied with the narrow streets and queer smells of the town, and spared no comment on these points while assisting her young mistress at her toilette. Having dressed, Margery passed into an antechamber, close to her bedroom, where breakfast was served. This repast consisted of a pitcher of new milk, another pitcher of wine, a dish of poached eggs, a tremendous bunch of water-cress, a large loaf of bread, and marchpanes —a sweet cake, not unlike the modern macaroon. Breakfast over, Margery put on her hood, and taking Alice with her, she sallied forth on an expedition to examine the neighbourhood of her new home. One of Lord Marnell's men-servants followed at a short distance, wearing a rapier, to defend his mistress in case of any assault being made upon her.

Lord Marnell's house was very near the country, and in a quiet and secluded position, being pleasantly situated in Fleet Street. Green fields lay between the two cities of London and Westminster. There was only one bridge across the river, that silver Thames, which ran, so clear and limpid, through the undulating meadows ; and the bridge was entirely built over, a covered way passing under the houses for wheeled vehicles. Far to the right rose the magnificent Palace of Westminster, a relic of the Saxon kings ; and behind it the grand old Abbey, and the strong, frowning Sanctuary ; while to the left glittered the walls and turrets of the White Tower, the town residence of royalty. Margery, however, could not see the whole of this as she stepped out of her house. What first met her eyes were the more detailed and less pleasant features of the scene. There were no causeways ; the streets, as a rule, would just allow of the progress of one vehicle, though a few of the principal ones would permit the passage of two ; and the pavements consisted of huge stones, not remarkable either for evenness or smoothness. A channel ran down the middle of the street, into which every housewife emptied her slops from the window, and along which dirty water, sewerage, straw, drowned rats, and mud, floated in profuse and odoriferous *melee*. Margery found it desirable to make considerable use of her pomander, a ball of various mixed drugs inclosed in a gold network, and emitting a pleasant fragrance when carried in the warm hand. As she proceeded along the streets which were lined with shops, the incessant cry of the shopkeepers standing at their doors, " What do you lack ? what do you lack ? " greeted her on every side. The vehicles were of two classes, as I have before observed —waggons and litters, the litters being the carriages of the fourteenth century ; but the waggons were by far the most numerous. Occasionally a lady of rank would ride past in her litter, drawn by horses whose trappings swept the ground ; or a knight, followed by a crowd of retainers, would prance by on his high-mettled charger. Margery spent the happiest day which she had passed since her marriage, in wandering about London, and satisfying her girlish curiosity concerning every place of which she had ever heard.

Lord Marnell frowned when Margery confessed, on her return, that she had been out to see London. It was not fit, he said, that she should go out on foot : ladies of rank were not expected to walk : she ought to have ordered out her litter, with a due attendance of retainers.

"But, my lord," said Margery, very naturally, "an't please you, I could not see so well in a litter."

Lord Marnell's displeased lips relaxed into a laugh, for he was amused at her simplicity ; but he repeated that he begged she would remember, now that she *had* seen, that she was no longer plain Mistress Margery Lovell, but Baroness Marnell of Lymington, and would behave herself accordingly. Margery sighed at this curtailment of her liberty, and withdrew to see where Alice was putting her dresses.

As it was approaching evening, Lord Marnell's voice called her down-stairs.

"If thou wilt see a sight, Madge," he said, good-naturedly, as she entered, " come quickly, and one will gladden thine eyes which never sawest thou before. The King rideth presently from the Savoy to the Tower."

Margery ran to the window, and saw a number of horses, decked, as well as their riders, in all the colours of the rainbow, coming up the street from the stately Savoy Palace, which stood, surrounded by green fields, in what is now the Strand.

"Which is the King's Grace, I pray you?" asked she, eagerly.

"He weareth a plain black hood and a red gown," answered her husband. "He rideth a white horse, and hath a scarlet footcloth, all powdered over with ostrich feathers in gold."

"What!" said Margery, in surprise, "that little, fair, goodly man, with the golden frontlet to his horse?"

"The very same," said Lord Marnell. "The tall, comely man who rideth behind him, on yon brown horse, and who hath eyes like to an eagle, is the Duke of Lancaster. 'John of Gaunt,' the folk call him, by reason that he was born at Ghent, in Flanders."

"And who be the rest, if I weary you not with asking?" said Margery, rather timidly.

"In no wise," answered he. "Mostly lords and noble gentlemen, of whom thou mayest perchance have heard. The Earl of Surrey is he in the green coat, with a red plume. The Earl of Northumberland hath a blue coat, broidered with gold, and a footcloth of the same. Yon dark, proud-looking man in scarlet, on the roan horse, is the Duke of Exeter,[1] brother to the King's Grace by my Lady Princess his mother, who was wed afore she wedded the Prince, whose soul God rest! Ah! and here cometh my Lord of Hereford, Harry of Bolingbroke,[2] the Duke of Lancaster's only son and heir—and a son and heir who were worse than none, if report tell truth," added Lord Marnell, in a lower tone. "Seest thou, Madge, yon passing tall man, with black hair, arrayed in pink cloth of silver?"[3]

"I see him well, I thank your good Lordship," was Margery's answer; but she suddenly shivered as she spoke.

"Art thou cold, Madge, by the casement? Shall I close the lattice?"

"I am not cold, good my Lord, I thank you," said Margery, in a different tone; "but I like not to look upon that man."

---

[1] Sir John Holland.   [2] Afterwards Henry IV.

[3] These descriptions are taken from the invaluable illuminations in Creton's *Histoire du Roy Richart Deux*, Harl. MS. 1319. Creton was a contemporary and personal friend of King Richard.

"Why so ? " asked Lord Marnell, looking down from his altitude upon the slight frail figure at his side. " Is he not a noble man and a goodly ? "

" I know not," answered Margery, still in a troubled voice. "There is a thing in his face for which I find not words, but it troubleth me."

"Look not on him, then," said he, drawing her away. She thanked him for his kindness in showing and explaining the glittering scene to her, and returned to her supervision of Alice.

A few days after this, the Prioress of Kennington, Lord Marnell's sister, came in her litter to see her young sister-in-law. Margery was surprised to find in her a lady so little resembling her country-formed idea of a nun. She wore, indeed, the costume of her order; but her dress, instead of being common serge or camlet, was black velvet; her frontlet and barb [1] were elaborately embroidered; her long gloves [2] were of white Spanish leather, delicately perfumed, and adorned with needlework in coloured silks; she wore nearly as many rings as would have stocked

[1] The frontlet and barb were pieces of white linen, the former worn over the forehead, the latter over the chin.

[2] Gloves were just becoming fashionable in the fourteenth century for common wear. Before that, they were rarely used except when the wearer carried a falcon on the wrist.

a small jeweller's shop, and from her girdle, set with the finest gems, were suspended a pomander richly worked in gold and enamel, a large silver seal, and a rosary, made of amethyst beads, holding a crucifix, the materials of which were alabaster and gold.

In those palmy days of Romanism in England, nuns were by no means so strictly secluded as now. They were present at all manner of festivities ; the higher class travelled about the country very much as they chose, and all of them, while retaining the peculiar shape and colour of the prescribed monastic costume, contrived to spend a fortune on the accessories and details of their dress. The Prioress of Kennington, as I have just described her, is a specimen of nearly all the prioresses and other conventual authorities of her day.

This handsomely-dressed lady was stiff and stately in her manner, and uttered, with the proudest mien, words expressive only of the most abject humility. "If her fair sister would come and see her at her poor house at Kennington, she would be right glad of so great honour." Margery replied courteously, but she had no desire to see much of the Prioress.

Lord Marnell took his wife to Court, and presented her to the King—the Queen was dead—and the

Duchess of Gloucester,[1] his aunt. The King spoke
to Margery very kindly, and won her good opinion
by so doing. The Duchess honoured her with a
haughty stare, and then "supposed she came from
the North ? " in a tone which indicated that she
considered her a variety of savage. The ladies in
waiting examined and questioned her with more
curiosity than civility ; and Margery's visit to Court
left upon her mind, with the single exception of King
Richard's kindness, a most unpleasant impression.

In the winter of 1396, King Richard brought home
a new queen, the Princess Isabelle of France, who
had attained the mature age of eight years. Margery
watched the little Queen make her entrance into
London. She was decked out with jewels, of which
she brought a great quantity over with her, and
fresh ones were presented to her at every place where
she halted. Alice, with round eyes, declared that
" the Queen's Grace's jewels must be worth a King's
ransom—and would not your good Ladyship wish
to have the like ? "

Margery shook her head.

" The only jewels that be worth having, good Alice,"
said she, " be gems of the heart, such like as meekness,

---

[1] Eleanor Bohu.

obedience, and charity. And in truth, if I were the chooser, there be many things that I would have afore jewels. But much good do they the Queen's Grace, poor child! and I pray God she rest not content with gauds of this earth."

Before that winter was over, one thing, worth more than the Queen's jewels in her eyes, was bestowed upon Margery. Something to take care of—something to love and live for. A little golden-haired baby, which became, so far as anything in this world could become so, the light and joy of her heart and soul.

Margery soon learned to value at its true worth the show and tinsel of London life. She never appeared again at Court but once, to pay her respects to the new Queen, who received her very cordially, seated on a throne by her husband. The small Queen of eight "hoped she was quite well, and thought that England was a very fine country." The king spoke to her as kindly as before, offered her ipocras[1] and spices, and on the close of the interview, took up his little Queen in his arms, and carried her out of the room. Margery had, indeed, no opportunity to visit the Court again; for the young Queen was

[1] A sweet wine or liqueur, generally served at the "void."

educated at Windsor, and very rarely visited London. And Lady Marnell, tired of the hollow glitter of high life, and finding few or none in her own sphere with whom she could complacently associate, went back with fresh zest to her baby and the book.

CHAPTER V.

THE BEGINNING OF THE END.

" All quick and troubled was his speech,
    And his face was pale with dread,
And he said, ' The king had made a law,
    That the book must not be read,—
For it was such fearful heresy,
    The holy abbot said.' "

—MARY HOWITT.

THREE years had passed since the events narrated in the last chapter, and Margery was now twenty-one years of age. She appeared older than she was, and her face wore an unnaturally pensive expression, which had been gradually settling itself there since the day of her marriage. She never laughed, and very rarely smiled, except when her eyes rested upon her little golden-haired Geoffrey, whom she had sought and obtained permission to name after her father. He was a bright, merry little fellow, perpetually in motion, and extremely fond of his mother, though he always shrank from and seemed to fear his father.

On a summer day in the year 1399, Margery sat in her bower, or boudoir, perusing the book. Lord Marnell was, as usual, at Court ; and little Geoffrey was running about his mother's apartments on what he doubtless considered important business. Suddenly, in the midst of her reading, a cry of pain from the child startled Margery. She sprang up, and ran to him ; and she found that in running about, he had contrived to fall down a step which intervened between the landing and the antechamber, whereby he had very slightly bruised his infantine arm, and very greatly perturbed his infantine spirit. Geoffrey was weeping and whining piteously, and his mother lifted him up, and carried him into her bedroom, where she examined the injured arm, and discovered that the injury consisted only of an almost imperceptible bruise. The child, however, still bewailed his misfortune ; and Lady Marnell, having applied some ointment to the sore place, sat down, and taking Geoffrey in her lap, she soothed and rocked him until he fell asleep, and forgot all about his bruised arm. The boy had been asleep about a quarter of an hour, when the recollection suddenly flashed upon Margery's mind that she had left the book open to all comers and goers, instead of putting it carefully away, as was her wont. She set down the child softly on the trussing-bed, (the curious name given by our forefathers to a piece of furniture which formed a sofa or travelling-bed at pleasure), and quietly opening the door into her bower, she saw—her husband standing on the hearth, with the book in his hand, and a very decided frown gathering on his countenance. The rustle of Margery's dress made Lord Marnell look up.

"What meaneth this, I pray you, mistress?" asked he, angrily.

There was no need, had Margery felt any disposition, to attempt further concealment. The worst that could come, had come.

"It is a book of mine," she quietly answered, "which I left here a short season agone, when the boy's cry started me."

"Hast read it?" asked Lord Marnell, no less harshly.

"I have read it many times, good my Lord."

"And I pray you for to tell me whence you had it, good my Lady?" said he, rather ironically.

Margery was silent. She was determined to bear the blame alone, and not to compromise either Pynson or Carew.

"Had you this book since you came hither?"

said Lord Marnell, varying the form of his question, when he saw she did not answer.

" No, my Lord.　I brought it with me from home."

And the word " home " almost brought the tears into her eyes.

" Your father—Sir Geoffrey—knew he thereof ? "

" He did," said Margery, " and rebuked me sharply therefor."

" He did well.　Why took he not the book from you ? "

" Because he showed it to Friar Andrew Rous, his and my confessor, who thought there was no harm in the book, and that I might safely retain the same."

" Then Friar Andrew Rous is the longest-eared ass I have lightly seen.　Whence got you this book ? "

" It is mine own writing.　I copied it."

" Whence had you it ? "

No answer.

" I say, whence had you this book ? " roared Lord Marnell.

" My Lord," said Margery, gently, but decidedly, " I think not that it needeth to say whence I had the same.　The book was lent unto me, whence I copied that one ; but I say not of whom it was lent unto me."

" You shall say it, and soon too ! " was the reply.
" This matter must not be let drop—it passeth into
the hands of holy Abbot Bilson. I will seek him
presently."

And so saying, Lord Marnell strode out of the
room, leaving Margery in a condition of intense terror.

That afternoon, as Margery sat in her bower, she
was informed that the Prioress of Kennington was
in the oaken chamber. Margery went down to her,
holding Geoffrey by the hand, and found her seated
on a settle, apparently preferring this more ancient
form of seat to a chair ; and wearing her veil low
over her face. The Prioress rose when Lady Marnell
entered, and threw back her heavy black veil, as she
advanced to greet her. Margery returned her salutation courteously, and then tried to induce Geoffrey
to go to his aunt—but Geoffrey hung back and would
not go. Margery did not attempt to force the child,
but sat down, and he attached himself to that particular
plait of her dress which was furthest from the Prioress.
The Prioress tried to propitiate him, by drawing
from her pocket a piece of linen, which, being unfolded,
revealed a placenta—a delicacy which the nuns of
several convents were specially famed for making,
and the nature of which will be better known to an

ordinary reader by the explanatory term cheese-cake. Geoffrey graciously accepted the placenta, but utterly declined all further intimacy. The expression of the Prioress's countenance suggested to Margery the idea that she had seen her brother, and had heard of the discovery of the book ; so that Margery was quite prepared for her remarking gravely, after her unsuccessful attempt to attract her little nephew—

" I heard this morn, fair sister, of a thing which did much trouble me."

" You mean," said Margery, simply, " of the discovering of a book in my chamber by my Lord my husband, the which did anger him ? "

" I rejoice that you take my meaning," answered the Prioress, in an even voice. " I meant that verily. I grieve much, fair sister, to hear from my fair brother that you have allied yourself unto those evil men which be known by the name of Lollards."

" I cry you mercy, holy mother," answered Margery, quietly, " I have allied myself unto no man. I know not a Lollard in the realm. Only I read that book— and that book, as you must needs wit, holy mother, containeth the words of the Lord Jesu. Is there hurt therein ? "

The Prioress did not directly answer this question.

She said, "If your elders,[1] fair sister, had shown the wisdom for to have put you in the cloister, you would have been free from such like temptations."

"Is it a temptation?" replied Margery. "Meseemeth, holy mother, that there be temptations as many in the cloister as in the world, only they be to divers sins: and I misdoubt that I should have temptation in the cloister, to the full as much as here."

"I cry you mercy, fair sister!" said the Prioress, with an air of superiority. "We have no temptations in our blessed retreat. Our rule saveth us, and our seclusion from the vanity of the world—and I pray you, what other evil can assail a veiled nun?"

Margery glanced at the heavy gold chain round the Prioress's neck, the multifarious rings on her fingers, and the costly jewels in her girdle, and rather doubted her testimony as to the utter absence of vanity in a veiled nun; but she contented herself with saying, "I trow, holy mother, that ye carry with you evil hearts into your cloister, as have all men without; and an evil heart within, and the devil without, need not outward matters whereon to form temptation. At least, I speak by mine own."

The Prioress looked rather shocked. "The evil

[1] Parents.

heart," answered she, "is governed and kept down in us by our mortifications, our almsgivings, our penances, our prayers, and divers other holy exercises."

"Ah, holy mother," said Margery, looking up, "can ye keep down by such means your evil hearts? I trow mine needeth more than that!"

"What mean you, fair sister?" inquired the Prioress.

"Nought less," replied Margery, "than the blood of the Lamb slain, and the grace of Christ risen, have I yet found, that would avail to keep down an evil heart!"

"Of force, fair sister, of force!" said the Prioress, coldly, "that is as well as said."

"Then I pray you, why said you it not?"

The Prioress rose. "I trust, fair sister," said she, without giving any reply to Margery's home question, "that you may see your error ere it be full late so to do."

"I trust," said Margery, as she followed her sister-in-law to the door, "that God will keep me in the true faith, whatsoever that be."

"Amen!" said the Prioress, her long black robe sweeping the steps as she mounted her litter.

"Is she gone?" lisped little Geoffrey, when his

mother returned. "Deff'y so glad! Deff'y don't like her!"

That evening Margery received a message from her husband, bidding her meet him and Abbot Bilson in the oaken chamber, and bring the book with her. She took the book from the table on which Lord Marnell had thrown it—no need to hide it any longer now—kissed little Geoffrey's sleeping forehead, as he lay in his cradle, and went down to the oaken chamber.

Lord Marnell, who, when angry, looked taller than ever, stood on the hearth with his arms folded. Abbot Bilson was seated in an arm-chair, with his cowl thrown back. He was a man of about sixty, with a finely-formed head, more bald than the tonsure would account for, and a remarkably soft, persuasive voice and manner. Had the Order of Jesuits existed at that time, Abbot Bilson might fitly have been the head of it. "His words were softer than oil, yet were they drawn swords."

"The Lady Marnell," said her husband to the Abbot as she entered, and the latter, without rising, saluted her with the benediction, "Peace be with thee, daughter."

" Where is the book ? " asked Lord Marnell, sternly, but not quite so angrily as he had spoken in the morning.

Margery passed it to him.

" See there, reverend father," said he, as he handed it to the Abbot. " What callest thou that ? "

The Abbot turned over the leaves, but the suavity of his manner suffered no change.

" A fine, clear scribe hath written this," remarked he, politely. " The Gospel according unto the blessed John, I ween, from the traduction of Master John Wycliffe, the parson of Lutterworth, who deceased a few years back. And our good brother Andrew Rous thought no harm of your keeping the book, my daughter ? "

" So he said," answered Margery, shortly.

" Ah ! But your father——? "

" Did not like thereof at the first ; but after that Father Rous had so said, he made no further matter."

" Ah ! of force. I conceive it fully. Your mother, good daughter ? "

" My mother spake not of the matter. She witteth not to read, and therefore knew not the book."

" Certes," said the abbot, with the most exquisite gentleness. Lord Marnell, who kept fidgeting up and down the room, seemed almost annoyed at the Abbot's extreme suavity.

" You had this book from a friend, methinks ? " resumed the Abbot.

" I cannot tell you, father, whence I had it," was Margery's firm reply.

The Abbot looked surprised.

" Did our brother Rous lend it you ? " he asked, his manner losing a small portion of its extraordinary softness.

" Nay."

" Some friend, then, belike ? Sir Ralph Marston, your good cousin ? or Master Pynson, the squire of my worthy knight your father ? "

Margery felt instantaneously that she was in the power of a very dangerous man. How he was endeavouring to ferret out admissions and denials which would afterwards stand him in good stead ! How came he, too, to know so much about her friends ? Had he been questioning Lord Marnell ? Margery's breath came short and fast, and she trembled exceedingly. She was annoyed with herself beyond measure, because, when the Abbot named Richard Pynson, she could not help a conscious blush in hearing him mention, not indeed the person who had actually lent her the book, but one who was concerned in the transaction. The Abbot saw the blush, though just then it did not suit his purpose to take notice of it.

"Well, well," said he, courteously, "we will not go further into that question at present. But you must wit, dear daughter, that this book containeth fearful heresy! Hath not our brother Rous taught you the same? Error of all kinds is therein, and weak women like unto you be not able, my child, for to separate in all cases this error from the truth wherewith, in these pernicious volumes, it is mingled. You are very young, daughter, and wit not yet all that the fathers of the Church can tell you, an' you be meek and humble in receiving of their teaching."

He ceased, evidently thinking that he had made an impression. He was quite prepared for a little pouting, and for earnest entreaties, and even passionate words; but the one thing for which he was not prepared he got in Margery's answer.

"I wis well, reverend father," she said, very quietly, "to the full as well as it list you to tell me, how young, and weak, and all unwitting I be. But I trow that Christ deceiveth not His children because they be weak; and that if I can any words at all conceive, I can His. Saith He not, '*If ony man wole do His wille,*

he schall knowe of the techinge' ?[1] Saith He not again,
'Seke ye Scripturis' ?[2] I pray you now, father, to whom
said He that ? Unto fathers of the Church ? Nay,
soothly, but unto Jews unbelieving—very heathens,
and no Christians. Moreover, saith He not again,
'He that dispisith me, and takith not my wordis, hath
him that schal juge him ; thilk word that I have spoken
schal deme him in the laste day' ?[3] I pray you, good
father, how shall I know the word that shall judge
me if I read it not ? Truly meseemeth that the despising
of His Word lieth more in the neglect thereof. Also
say you that this book containeth heresy and evil
teaching. Good father, shall Christ the Son of God
teach evil ? Doth God evil ? Will God deceive them
that ask Him truth ? Knoweth He not as much as
fathers of the Church ? Nay truly, good father, I
trust that you wot not fully what you have said.
He is *'weye, treuthe, and lyf ; no man cometh to the*
Fadir but by Him.' "[4]

Abbot Bilson, for once in his life, was completely
dumbfounded. He looked silently at Lord Marnell.

"I pray you see now, reverend father," said Lord
Marnell, angrily, "how the teaching of this book

---

[1] John vii. 17. [2] John v. 39.
[3] John xii. 48. [4] John xiv. 6

hath leavened yon girl's talk! Is it a small evil, Madge, to turn upon thy teacher when he teacheth thee of wisdom, with sayings picked up from a book? Art not ashamed?"

"No, my Lord, I am no wise shamed," answered she; "for the reverend father teacheth me the words of men, and the words of my book be the words of Christ; and when Christ and men come to warring, I trow there is small doubt as to who shall be the winner."

The Abbot sat mutely gazing at Margery. Her face, usually so calm and pale, was lighted up, as she spoke, with a light not of this world; and he could not comprehend it. Had she asked pardon, he could have soothed her; had she lamented and bewailed, he might have promised her many things to comfort her; had she spoken bitterly or passionately, he might have commanded her silence. But this conduct of hers, so quiet, yet so decided—so gentle, but so uncompromising—puzzled him extremely. He only saw the exterior, and he could not discover that wherein her great strength lay.

"My Lord Marnell," he said, in a perplexed tone, "I would speak with you. Good lady, will you give us leave?"

Margery rose, and, courtesying, quitted the room at once; but she took the book with her, and nobody prevented her from doing so.

"My Lord," said the Abbot, when she was gone, "I am bewildered utterly. I know not what to do with this girl. Never the like of her saw I before, and my experience is baffled. But meseemeth that the best thing is to treat her gently at the first; and if she relent not, *then*——"

The sentence was left unfinished, but Lord Marnell understood it.

CHAPTER VI.

NEWS FROM HOME.

" There are briars besetting every path,
    That call for patient care ;
There is a cross in every lot,
    And an earnest need for prayer ;
But a lowly heart that leans on Thee
    Is happy anywhere."

—MISS WARING.

IT was a lovely, clear, moonlight night, 'and the streets of London were hushed and still. By the light of the moon might be discerned a man in traveller's dress, walking slowly along Fleet Street, and looking up at the houses, as if uncertain which of them would prove the one he sought. The traveller, though he looks much older, and his face wears a weary, worn expression, we recognise as our old friend Richard Pynson. Suddenly, in the midst of his search, Richard stopped and looked up. From an oriel window, directly above his head, a faint sound of singing reached him—an air which he instantly recognised as "The Palmer's hymn," sung

by the pilgrims to Jerusalem on their journey to the
Holy Land.   The voice of the singer, though low, was
so clear, that the words of the hymn were floated
distinctly to his ear.

> "Holy City, happy City,
>   Built on Christ, and sure as He,
> From my weary journeying,
>   From the wastes, I cry to thee;
> Longing, sighing, hasting, crying,
>   Till within thy walls I be.
> Ah! what happy, happy greeting
>   For the guests thy gates who see!
> Ah! what blessed, blessed meeting
>   Have thy citizens in thee!
> Ah! those glittering walls how fair,
>   Jasper shene and ruby blee.
> Never harm, nor sin, nor danger,
>   Thee can tarnish, crystal sea;
> Never woe, nor pain, nor sorrow,
>   Thee can enter, City free!"[1]

The voice ceased, and Richard Pynson, without
any further doubt or trouble, applied at once for
admittance at the gate of the house whence the music
had issued.   He could never mistake the voice of
Margery Lovell.   The old porter, half asleep, came to

[1] Any reader acquainted with mediæval hymns will recognise
in this—
> "Urbs cœlestis! urbs beata!
>   Super petram collocata."

I have translated a few lines of the hymn for the benefit of the
English reader; but my heroine must be supposed to sing it in
the original Latin.

the gate, and, sentinel-like, inquired, "Who goes there?"

"A friend, a messenger from Dame Lovell, who would fain have speech, if he may, of the Lady Marnell."

As soon as the porter heard the name of Dame Lovell, he threw open the gate. "Enter, friend." The ponderous gate swung to again, and the old man slowly preceded Richard through the archway to the door of the house, and up the wide staircase. He ushered him into a room panelled with oak, where he stirred up the decaying embers of the fire, requested him to be seated, and left the room. At the door of the adjoining chamber, Richard heard him softly whisper,

"Mistress Alice! Mistress Alice!"

A gentle movement in the room followed, and then Richard heard the familiar voice of Alice Jordan.

"Hush! good Christopher," said she, in a low tone; "the boy sleepeth at last—wake him not. What wouldst?"

"There is here a messenger from Lovell Tower, who would have speech of my Lady."

On hearing this, Alice came forward at once into the oaken chamber where Richard sat.

"Ah! Master Pynson!" she said, "is it you!

My Lady will be right fain to see you—but you come at an evil hour."

"How so ? " asked Richard, quickly.

"My Lady is watching this livelong night by the cradle of the young master, who is sore sick—we fear nigh unto death.   The child is in grievous disease, [1] and cannot sleep ; and her good Ladyship hath been singing unto him, I ween, for to soothe him to rest. Her voice hushed as you came, wherefore I count that the boy sleepeth."

"What aileth the poor child ? " inquired Richard.

"My Lady counteth that he got him an ill rheum when we departed hence for my Lord his house of plesance, [2] for to sweeten. [3] Howsoever that be, he is now grievous sick."

"The Lady Marnell herself is well ? "

"Alas ! " replied Alice, "I ween she is little better than the child. She hath been in sore trouble of late, wherefore it is no marvel. There be rumours of accusations for heresy out against her, and my Lord

---

[1] Restlessness, uneasiness.   [2] Country house.

[3] " Sweetening " was a process to which our forefathers were compelled by their want of drains, and consisted in leaving a house entirely empty for a time, to have the windows opened, the rushes renewed, and to admit of a general purification. Families who had the means generally " went to sweeten " at least every summer.

is ill angered towards her. Well, God witteth, and God keep her! You will see how evil[1] she looketh an' she come to speak with you, and I trow that she will when I give her to wit who is here."

So saying, Alice returned to the room she had quitted, and for some minutes Richard heard nothing more. Then the door re-opened, and a lady entered the chamber.

Was *that* Margery Lovell? Never, surely, were hers that feeble step, that worn, wan, white face, that dark ring round the eyes, telling of weary vigils, and of bitter weeping! But the smile of welcome was Margery Lovell's own, and the gesture, as she came forward quickly, holding out both hands, was hers also; though the smile died away in an instant, and the worn, wearied look came back instead.

" Dear, good friend! " she said, " how it gladdeth me to see you! You come straightway from Lovell Tower? My father and mother be well? And Mistress Katherine, and Cicely, and all the maidens? And Lyard, and old Beaudesert? (naming her palfrey and the watchdog). And all mine old friends—Sir Ralph Marston, and Master Carew? "

Richard smiled a grave, almost mournful smile.

[1] Ill.

"You ask too many questions, good my Lady, to be answered in a breath. But Dame Lovell is in health, and greets you well by me, bidding you be assured ever of her love and blessing."

"And my father? O Master Pynson, my father! my father!"

She sat down, and buried her face in her hands, and wept; for though Richard had made no answer in words, his face told his tidings too unmistakably. Sir Geoffrey Lovell was dead. After a time Margery looked up whiter and more wan than ever, and begged to know the particulars of her father's death. Richard informed her that Sir Geoffrey had been taken ill three days only before he died; they had immediately summoned Master Carew, who was a physician, and who had pronounced that since he could not live many days, it would be useless to send for his daughter, who could not possibly reach Lovell Tower in time to see him alive. Dame Lovell was well in health, but had quite lost her old cheerfulness, and appeared to feel her husband's death very acutely. It had been arranged that Friar Andrew should remain with Dame Lovell as her confessor. As to himself, Richard said that he should of course return to his father for a time, until he could by some act of bravery or special favour receive the honour of knighthood; but he did not like to say anything to Dame Lovell about leaving her, so long as he saw that he was of any use to her, as he knew that she regarded him in the light of an adopted son, and had especially seemed to cling to him since Margery's departure.

Margery replied that she would have requested for him the favour of knighthood in a moment at the hands of Lord Marnell, but she did not like to ask him for anything so long as he was displeased with her.

Richard inquired after Lord Marnell. Margery said he was well, and was with the King at Havering-atte-Bower: but talking about him seemed to increase her look of weariness and woe. She turned the subject by inquiring again about her old friends. Cicely and the maids, Richard told her, were well; but old Beaudesert always howled whenever he was asked for Madge; and Lyard would stand switching his tail in the meadow, and looking wistfully at the house for the young mistress whom he must never see again.

"You miss me, then, all?" said Margery, mournfully.

"You will never know how sore," was Richard's answer.

Another pause ensued—there seemed some strange constraint between them—and then Richard asked—

"And what tidings take I home, good my Lady? Dame Lovell bade me have a care to ask how you fared, and the child. I grieve to hear from Alice Jordan that *he* fareth but evil, and for *you*——" He smiled the same grave smile.

"Well—*well*, Master Pynson," said Margery, quickly. "I fare well. I cannot go where is not Christ, and where He is, howsoever I fare, I must needs fare well. And for the child—come and see him."

She led the way noiselessly to the adjoining room. Little Geoffrey lay in Alice's arms in a heavy sleep. His breathing was very quick and short, and his face flushed and fevered. Richard stood looking silently at him for a few minutes, and then returned with Margery to the oaken chamber. She offered him refreshments, but he declined them. He had supped, he said, already; and ere breakfast-time, he looked to be on his way back to the North. Margery wrote a short letter to Dame Lovell, and intrusted it to him; and then she sat by the table, wearily resting her head upon her hand.

"I pray you, good my Lady," said Richard, suddenly, breaking the spell that seemed to bind them,

" what meaneth this bruit [1] of heresy that I hear of you ? "

Margery looked up with a strange light in her eyes.

" You remember, I trow, asking Master Carew for to lend me yon book ?—and wending with me to hear Master Sastre's homily ? "

" I mind it well."

" *That* meaneth it. That because I read Christ's words, and love them, and do them, so far as in my poor power lieth, the charge of heresy is laid at my door. And I ween they will carry it on to the end."

" *The end ?* " said Richard, tremblingly,—for he guessed what that meant, and the idea of Margery being subjected to a long and comfortless imprisonment, was almost more than he could bear. His own utter powerlessness to save her was a bitter draught to drink.

" Aye, the end ! " she said, with the light spreading all over her face. " Mind you not how Master Sastre asked us if we could sue the Lamb along the weary and bitter road ? Is it an evil thing to sue the Lamb, though He lead over a few rugged stones which be lying in the path ? Nay, friend, I am ready for the suing, how rough soever the way be."

[1] Noise, rumour.

Richard sat looking at her in silence. He had always thought her half an angel, and now he thought her so more than ever.

"I trow you know these things, good friend?" said Margery, with her sad, faint smile. "You know, is it not, how good is Christ?"

"I am assaying for to know," answered Richard, huskily. "I have been a-reading of Master Carew's book, since I found you counted it so great a thing. Oft-times have Master Carew and I sat reading of that book whenever I could make an errand unto his neighbourhood; and he hath taught me many things. But I cannot say yet that I be where you be, Mistress Margery," he added, calling her by the old familiar title, "or that I know Christ as friendly as you seem to know Him."

"Then," said Margery, earnestly, "let not go your grasp till you have fast hold of Him. Ah! what matter how soon or how sore cometh the end, if '*whanne He hath loued Hise that ben in the world, into the ende He loueth them.*' [1] O dear friend, count not anything lost if thou keepest Christ His love! If He shall come unto thee and say of aught by which thou settest store, as He did say unto Peter, '*Louest*

---

[1] John xiii. 1.

thou me more than these?' let thine answer be his, *'Ghe, Lord, Thou woost that I loue Thee!'* [1] Oh count not aught too rare or too brave for to give Christ! *'He that loueth his lyf schal leese it; and he that hatith his lyf in this world, kepith it unto everlastinge lyf.'* [2] No man loseth by that chepe [3] of life worldly for life everlasting. Never shall the devils have leave to say, 'Behold here a man who hath lost by Christ!'"

"Must we needs give Christ *all?*" said Richard, in an unsteady tone.

"Is there a thing that thou wouldst keep from Him?—a thing that thou lovest more than thou lovest Him? Then it will be no marvel that thou shouldst lose the same. Trust me, if His heart be set on thee, He will either have thy heart away from it by thy good will, or will have it away from thy heart by bitter rending and sorrow. And alas for that man who hath no portion in Christ His heart!"

Richard answered almost in a whisper, and bent forward to take Margery's hand as he did so. The spell was fully broken now.

"There was only one thing, and He hath taken it. Margery, I loved *you.* I had given readily all else

---

[1] John xxi. 15.   [2] John xii. 25.

[3] Exchange, bargain.

but you. And I trow you will count it but a sorry [1] giving, wherein the heart goeth not with the hands."

She turned her head hastily away, and made no answer; but he felt her hand grow deathly cold in his own. He dropped it, and rose—and so did she. She went with him to the door; and there, as she offered her hand for a farewell greeting, she spoke—

"Richard, God hath parted thee and me, and whatsoever God doth He doth well. If it were as thou sayest, there was need thereof. When children come home to their father's house from afar, I trow they fall not a-bewailing that they had not leave to come in company. And if only we may clasp hands at the gate of the *Urbs Beata*, I trow well that we shall count it no great matter, good friend, that we saw but little the one of the other on the journey!"

Richard kissed her hand, and then she drew it from him, and softly passed into her darkened nursery. For a moment he stood looking after her. "Please God, we will, Margery!" he said to himself, at length. Then he ran lightly down the stairs, and old Christopher

[1] Poor, unworthy.

rose at the sound of his step to open the door for him.

And so Richard Pynson and Margery Marnell parted, never more to speak to each other on this side of the Happy City.

CHAPTER VII.

BEREAVEMENT, BUT NOT DEATH.

" Take from me anything Thou wilt,
But go not Thou away ! "

LITTLE Geoffrey slowly recovered from the illness which had brought him to death's door, and though able to run about the house, he was still far from perfect health, when Margery received orders to prepare for another interview with Abbot Bilson. She rightly divined that this would be more stormy than the last. Abbot Bilson came now fully prepared, and not alone. He was accompanied by Archbishop Arundel, a man of violent passions, and a bitter persecutor of all whom he conceived to lean to the opinions of Wycliffe. When Margery entered the room, and saw the Archbishop, she trembled, as well she might. She meekly knelt and asked their blessing—the manner in which priests were commonly greeted. The Abbot gave his, saying, "May God bless thee, and lead thee unto the truth!" "Amen!" responded Margery. Arundel, however, refused his benediction until he had inquired into the matter.

"Be seated, my daughter!" said the Abbot. Margery obeyed.

"Holy Church, daughter, hath been sore aggrieved by thine evil doing. She demandeth of thee an instant yielding of yon heretical and pernicious book, the which hath led thee astray; and a renunciation of thy heresy; the which done, thou shalt receive apostolic absolution and benediction."

"I know not, reverend father, what ye clepe[1] heresy. Wherein have I sinned?"

"In the reading of yon book, and in thy seldom confession. Moreover, I trow thou holdest with the way of John Wycliffe, yon evil reprobate!" replied the Archbishop.

"I cry you mercy, reverend fathers. I take my belief from no man. I crede[2] the words of Christ as I find the same written, and concern not myself with Master Wycliffe or any other. I know not any Lollards, neither have I allied myself unto them."

The Archbishop and the Abbot both looked at Lord Marnell—a mute inquiry as to whether Margery spoke the truth.

---

[1] Call.   [2] Believe.

" I ween it is so, reverend fathers," said he. " I wis nought of my wife her manner of living ere I wedded her, but soothly sithence[1] she came hither, I know of a surety that she hath never companied with any such evil persons as be these Lollards."

" Hold you *not* with the way of Wycliffe, daughter ? " inquired the Abbot.

" I wis not, reverend father," answered she, " for of a truth I know not wherein it lieth. I hold that which I find in the book ; and I trow an' I keep close by the words of Christ, I cannot stray far from truth."

" The words in yon book be no words of Christ ! " said Arundel. " That evil one Wycliffe, being taught of the devil, hath rendered the holy words of the Latin into pernicious heresy in English."

" I pray you then, father, will you give me the book in Latin, for I wis a little the Latin tongue, and moreover I can learn of one that hath the tongues to wit better the same."

This was not by any means what Arundel intended, and it raised his anger.

" I will not give thee the Latin ! " exclaimed he. " I forbid thee to read or learn the same, for I well know thou wouldst wrest it to thine evil purposes."

---

[1] Since.

" How can you put a right meaning to the words, my daughter ? " mildly suggested the Abbot.

" I know well that I could in no wise do the same," replied Margery, humbly, " had I not read the promise of Christ Jesu that He would send unto His own ' *thilk Spyryt of treuthe*,' who should ' *teche them al treuthe*,'[1] wherefore by His good help I trust I shall read aright."

" That promise was given, daughter, unto the holy apostles."

" It was given, reverend father, unto weak men and evil, else Peter had never denied his Master, ne[2] had all of them left Him and taken to flight, when the servants of the bishops[3] laid hold on Him. I wis that I have an evil heart like as they had, but meseemeth that mine is not worser than were theirs, wherefore I count that promise made unto myself also."

" Thou art lacking in meekness, Madge," said Lord Marnell.

" I trust not so, good my Lord ; but an' if I be, I pray God to give it to me."

---

[1] John xvi. 13.　　　　　　　　[2] Neither.

[3] Wycliffe always renders " Bisschopis " the word translated " chief priests " in the authorised version.

" Give up the book, Madge ! " said her husband, apparently desirous to allay the storm which he had raised, " and thou shalt then receive absolution, and all will go well."

" I will give up the book, my Lord, in obedience to you," replied Margery, " for I wis well that wives be bounden to obey their husbands ; and soothly it is no great matter, for I know every word therein. But under your good leave, my Lord, the truth which this book hath taught me, neither you nor any other man shall have power to take from me, for it is of God, and not of men ! "

She drew the book from her pocket—ladies wore much larger pockets in those days than they now do— kissed it, and handed it to her husband.

" Thou hast well done, Madge ! " said Lord Marnell, more kindly than before, as he passed the book to the Archbishop. Arundel, with a muttered curse upon all evil teaching, took the book from Lord Marnell with his hand folded in the corner of his gown, as if he thought its very touch would communicate pollution, and flung it into the fire. The fire was a large one, and in a minute the volume was consumed. Margery watched the destruction of her treasure with swimming eyes.

"Burn, poor book !" she said, falteringly, "and as thy smoke goeth up to God, leave it tell Him that the reading and the loving of His Word is accounted a sin by those who ought to be His pastors."

"Woman, wilt not hear the truth ?" cried Arundel.

"Truly, father, I have heard it, and it shall rest with me unto my dying day. But I trow that if your teaching were truth, ye had never burned with fire the Word of Christ, who hath power, if ye repent not, to consume you also with the like !"

"Told I not thee that the evil book which I gave to the fire was not Christ His Word, but the work of the devil ?"

"Yea, truly ; and the like said the heathen Jews, ' *Wher we seyen not wel that thou art a Samaritan, and hast a deuel ?* ' But I find not that their saying the same made it ever the truer. What saith Christ in answer ? ' *I haue not a deuel ; but I honoure my Fadir, and ye han unhonourid me.* ' "[1]

"My daughter," said the Abbot, with even more than his usual gentleness, "I misdoubt greatly that you be obstinate in your error. And if this be so, we shall have necessity of deeds the which we should sore lament. You wit, doubtless, that in case you

[1] John viii. 48, 49.

continue thus obstinate, you will be had up afore the King's Grace's Council ? "

" I am ready," answered Margery.

" You wit also," pursued the Abbot, no less gently, " that you may be sentenced unto close prison for such time as pleaseth the King's Grace ? "

" I am ready," said Margery again.

Her examiners looked surprised.

" Moreover," continued the Abbot, in a softer tone than ever, " wit you that we can allow you no longer to have the charge and teaching of your son, who must needs be instructed in the true faith ? "

The end of the reverend fathers was at length reached. The quiet words of the Abbot produced an effect which the furious abuse of the Archbishop had been unable to accomplish. A cry of mingled terror, anguish, and despair, broke from poor Margery's lips.

" Ye could not—ye could not be so cruel ! " she sobbed. " Take from me all I have in this world— comfort, freedom, yea, life—only leave me my child ! "

" Thou seest what thou hast brought on thyself ! " said Arundel. " How can we, being the ministers of God His truth, suffer the mind of yon innocent child to be poisoned with like evil doctrine ? "

"Doth God part the child from the mother?" faltered Margery. "This is none of His doing. My darling! my darling!"

Lord Marnell pitied his wife. Her agony touched all that was soft and gentle in his not too soft heart.

"Well, well, Madge!" he said, kindly; "I will see that thy child is not taken from thee, if thou wilt obey these reverend fathers in confessing of thine error, and wilt humbly beg absolution at their hands."

Margery looked up at her husband with an expression of unutterable gratitude beaming in her eyes— but the moment she heard his IF, her face fell instantly.

"I conceive you, good my Lord," she said, mournfully, "howsoever I thank you. You will give me back my darling, IF I will deny that I hold Christ His truth. I cannot. I dare not!"

"'Christ His truth,' persist you in calling your heresy?" cried Arundel, in a fury. "Choose, then, quickly, for the last time, betwixt 'Christ His truth' and your child!"

She shivered from head to foot as if an ague-fit were on her, and her sobs almost mounted to a scream. No heart that had any pretension to humanity could have helped pitying her. Her husband did pity her; but Arundel was carried away by passion, and Bilson had no heart. Through all this tempest, however agonised, firm and unwavering came the answer—

" CHRIST ! "

Arundel, rising, ordered her to kneel. Margery knelt down on the hearth, her hands clasped on her breast, and her eyes looking up to heaven. Solemnly, and with all that terrific majesty which the Church of Rome so well knows how to put into her threats and denunciations, the Archbishop cited her to appear before the council on the 17th day of the following September. In the meantime she was to be confined in one of the State dungeons. Arundel graciously added that he would give her the remainder of that day to make her preparations. Lord Marnell here interposed, and begged the Archbishop to reconsider his decision. He had anticipated Margery's examination by the council, and possibly her being sentenced to a term of imprisonment, but he had not bargained for this previous incarceration. Arundel bluntly refused to alter his sentence.

Margery raised her tearful eyes to Lord Marnell. " My Lord," she said, " and you, reverend fathers, I have one small thing to ask of you. I pray you deny me not."

" What is it, Madge ? " asked Lord Marnell.

"My good Lord," she said, pleadingly, "suffer
me to take one last kiss of my child, ere ye take me
where I shall see him no more!"

The Abbot seemed disposed to grant Margery's
petition, though the Archbishop demurred; but
Lord Marnell settled the matter by authoritatively
commanding that the mother should be permitted
to take leave of her child. Arundel, with rather a
bad grace, gave way on this secondary point. Margery
was then dismissed.

She went up-stairs as if she were walking in a dream,
and found Alice hiding behind the door for the amusement of little Geoffrey, who was in high glee. Margery
stood a moment on the threshold, looking at them,
and mournfully thinking that it was the last time she
would ever look on that sunny little face, or hear that
silvery laugh. As she stood there, Alice caught sight
of her mistress, and her share of the mirth ceased
instantly.

"My Lady! my Lady! what have you, I pray
you tell me? You look as if sentence of death had
been passed on you!"

Margery passed her hand dreamily across her
brow.

"Sentence, good Alice, of the evil which is in

death!" she said, softly, "and henceforth death must needs be a glad thing. But that is to come yet."

She sat down, and took the child on her knee, and he nestled his little golden head into her bosom. For a few minutes she rocked herself and him to and fro in silence, but at length her voice came, and though it trembled a little, it was almost as quiet and silvery as usual.

"Geofffey, dost love me?"

"Yes, mother, very much."

"Poor child! how wilt do without me!"

"Go you hence, mother?"

"Yes, my child, I go hence. Geoffrey, wilt mind ever what I now say unto thee? Wilt never, never forget it, but ever keep it fresh and shene, and think thereof whenever thou dost think of me?"

"Yes, mother, I shan't forget."

"Alice, thou wilt help him to remember, good lass, if thou be not taken from him."

"That will I, good my Lady," said Alice, sobbing, and only comprehending that something painful had happened.

"Geoffrey, darling, thou wilt be a good child to thy father?"

"I'll try, mother, but—he frighteth me."

Margery sighed heavily.

"List me now, my heart. Dost remember what I told thee about Jesus Christ?"

Geoffrey answered that he did.

"Right, my heart. And lovest Jesus Christ, who died for thee?"

"Yes, mother, I love Him and you."

The child's innocent answer nearly upset Margery's half-assumed calmness. She rocked him a minute longer in silence. "Remember, mine own sweet heart, ever that nothing but Jesus can save thee. Thou canst not save thyself. Beg of Him with all thine heart that He will save thee, and love Him all thy life long, even unto *the end*."

She ceased an instant.

"Now, sweet heart, kiss me. Give me a brave kiss, mine own—it is the last. Never shall we kiss again till we kiss in the Happy City! Fare-thee-well, dearly beloved! God have thee in His holy keeping! God teach thee what I cannot—what I by reason of mine ignorance know not, or what thou by reason of thy tender years canst not yet conceive. God forgive thee thy sins, and help thee in all trouble and woe, and bring thee to that blessed home where I shall see thee again, and where they sin not, nor grieve, neither part any more!"

. Margery gently detached herself from the child's embrace, and set him down. She desired Alice to take him away, and then to return and assist her in matters respecting which she would tell her particulars when she should have removed the child. She stood looking after the boy as Alice led him away, and he turned his head to say, "God be wi' ye!"[1]

"Never again! never again!" said Margery to herself in a half-whisper. "The worst part of death is over! I have nothing left now but Christ."

[1] The farewell phrase which has in modern times been shortened into "good-bye."

CHAPTER VIII.

A LODGING ON THE COLD GROUND.

"Christ is at hand to scorn or bless—
Christ suffers in our strife."
—*Christian Year.*

IN the evening, as previously ordered, Margery quitted Marnell Place in her litter for her prison in the Tower. The jailer stared at her, as Abbot Bilson, who accompanied her, gave her into his charge, and whisperingly asked the reason for which she was to be incarcerated.

"Heresy, good friend."

"Heresy!" said the jailer, staring more than ever. "What pity for one so marvellous young! Poor lady! it sorroweth me!"

When Margery was at length locked in, she had time to look round her prison. It was a small, square, white-washed cell, completely unfurnished; all the furniture had to be brought from Marnell Place. Not much was allowed. A mattress and blanket by

114

way of bed, a stool, and a crucifix, were the only articles permitted. The barred window was very small, and very high up. Here Margery was to remain until September. The days rolled wearily on. Lord Marnell occasionally visited her; but not often, and he was her sole visitor. The jailer, for a jailer, was rather kind to his prisoner, whom he evidently pitied; and one day he told her, as he brought her the prison allowance for supper, that "strange things" were taking place in the political world. There was a rumour in London that "my Lord of Hereford" had returned to England before his period of banishment was over, and had possessed himself of the person of King Richard at Flint Castle.

"What will he do?" asked Margery.

"Soothly I wis not," answered the jailer. "I trow he will make himself king. Any way, I trust it may hap for your Ladyship's good, for it is the wont to release prisoners at the beginning of a new reign."

Shortly after that, Henry of Bolingbroke fulfilled the jailer's prediction, so far as regarded his kingship. He led Richard in triumph through London, with every dishonour and indignity which his own evil nature could devise; then consigned him to Ponte-fract to die. and sat down on his throne. *How* Richard died, Henry best knew. Thus closed the life and reign of that most ill-treated and loving-hearted man, at the early age of thirty-three. The little Queen, a widow at-eleven, was sent back to France —her matchless collection of jewels being retained by Henry. Few men have had more reason to describe themselves as Henry IV. does in his will—" I, Henry, *sinful wretch.*" [1]

The change of monarchs, however, brought no change for Lady Marnell. If anything, it was the worse for her ; for Abbot Bilson was a personal friend of the new King, who was far more violently opposed to the Lollards than his predecessor had been.

On the 16th of September, 1400, Lord Marnell was just quitting Margery's cell, when the jailer admitted Abbot Bilson, who courteously greeted Lord Marnell, and replied rather more coldly to the salutation of his prisoner.

" Good morrow, my Lord. Have you induced this wretched girl to see the error of her ways ? "

[1] Henry had previously conspired against the King three times, and had even plotted the death of his own father. His father sentenced him to death, and if Richard had not interposed, Henry would not have lived to depose his benefactor. " How true is the saying," cried poor Richard in his agony, " that we have no greater enemy than the man whom we save from the gallows ! "—See Creton's MS. Bibl. Imp. 8448-2 *Ambassades.*

"I assayed it not," said Lord Marnell, somewhat sulkily. "Farewell, Madge,—I will see thee again ere long."

"Farewell, good my Lord," said Margery, and for the first time in her life she was sorry to see her husband go. The truth was, that Lord Marnell felt so much vexed with his spiritual advisers, that he was seriously afraid, if he remained, of saying something which might cause his own imprisonment. The jailer looked the door after him, and the Abbot and Margery were left together.

"You have had time, daughter, to think over your sin, in penitence and prayer. Are you yet conscious that you have committed a grievous sin?"

"No, father."

"No are?[1] I grieve to hear it. Fear you not the ban of Holy Church?"

"I fear it not, so Christ confirm it not; He did warn me afore of the same. '*Thei schulen make ghou withouten the synagogis ; but the our cometh, that ech man that sleeth ghou deme that he doith seruyse to God.*'"[2]

"Cease thy endless quotations from Scripture!" cried the Abbot, waxing wroth, and forgetting his civilities.

---

[1] *i.e.*, Are you not ?   [2] John xvi. 2.

But Margery only replied by another—

" ' *He that is of God herith the wordis of God ; therefore ye heren not for ye be not of God.*' " [1]

" Take the curse of the Church, miserable reprobate ! " cried Bilson, losing all command of himself, and smiting her in the face.

" Take you heed," was the answer, " that you bring not on yourself the curse of Christ, who is the Head and Lord of the Church, for He suffereth not lightly that His sheep be ill handled."

" Aroint thee, sorceress ! " said the abbot.

" I am no sorceress," replied Margery, quietly, " neither do I use evil arts ; I speak unto you in the words of Christ—bear you the sin if you will not hear. But lo ! it is even that which is written, ' *He hath blyndid her yghen,* [2] *and he hath maad hard the herte of hem ; that thei see not with yghen, and undirstonde with herte, and that thei be conuertid, and I heele hem.*' " [3]

The abbot could bear no more. He struck her furiously—a blow which stretched her senseless on the stone floor of the cell. Having by this primitive means silenced Margery's " endless quotations," he let himself out with a private key.

[1] John viii. 47.　　　　[2] Their eyes.
[3] John xii. 40.

When Lord Marnell returned to the prison that evening, he found Margery in what he supposed to be a swoon. He summoned the jailer, and through him sent for a physician, who applied restoratives, but told Lord Marnell at once that Margery had fallen, and had received a heavy blow on the head. By the united care of the physician and her husband, she slowly returned to consciousness : not, however, fully so at first, for she murmured, " Mother ! " When Lord Marnell bent over her and spoke to her, she suddenly recognised him as if awaking from a dream. Yes, she replied to their inquiries, she had certainly fallen, and she thought she had hurt her head ; but she would not tell them that the cause of the fall was a passionate blow from the Abbot's hand. The physician asked when her examination was to take place ; and on Lord Marnell replying, " To-morrow," he shook his head, and said she would not be able to appear.

" Oh aye, aye, let me go ! " said Margery, " I would not have delay therein. I shall be better by morn, and—— "

But as she spoke she fainted away, and the doctor, turning to Lord Marnell, said—

" She is no wise fit for it, poor lady ! The inquiry

must needs be delayed, and the blame thereof be mine own."

"Then I pray you," replied Lord Marnell, "to say the same unto the council; for they heed not me."

He answered that he would go to them as soon as he thought that his patient required no further professional assistance. Margery seemed better shortly, and Master Simon, for such was the doctor's name, repaired at once to the council charged with the examination of prisoners accused of heresy, and told them that their State prisoner, the Lady Marnell, was very ill in her dungeon, and would not be able to appear before them for at least some weeks to come. Arundel, who presided, only laughed. The doctor insisted.

"Why," said he, "the poor lady is sickening for a fever; let her alone: how can a woman light-headed answer questions upon doctrine and heresy?"

The council, governed by Arundel, still seemed unwilling to grant the prayer; when, to the surprise of every one present, Abbot Bilson, the principal witness for the Crown, rose and supported the petition. The puzzled council accordingly granted it. Arundel was very much under Bilson's influence, and Bilson had a private reason for his conduct, which will presently appear.

So the examination was adjourned until February, and Margery, released for the moment from the struggle with her enemies, was left to combat the fever which had seized her. Lord Marnell and Master Simon begged for an order of the council to remove poor Margery home, the latter asserting that she would never recover in the Tower. The council refused this application. They then requested that one of her waiting-women should be allowed to attend her, and that bedding and linen, with such other necessaries as Master Simon might deem fit, might be supplied to the prisoner from her own house. The council, after a private consultation among its members, thought fit to grant this reasonable prayer.

Alice Jordan was made very happy by an order from Lord Marnell to attend her sick mistress. Everything that Marnell Place could furnish, which Master Simon did not absolutely forbid,—and Master Simon was easy of persuasion—was lavished on the white-washed cell in the Tower. Alice, however, was carefully searched every time she passed in and out of the Tower, to see that she supplied no books nor writing-materials to the prisoner, nor took any letters

from her.   Poor Margery ! the care was needless, for
she was just then as incapable of writing as if she had
never been taught.

Margery's illness lasted even longer than Master
Simon had anticipated.   On a dark, cold winter night,
when snow was falling thickly outside the prison,
and a low rushlight burned on the table, dimly lighting
up the narrow cell, Margery unexpectedly whispered,
" Who is there ? "

" I, dear mistress—Alice Jordan."

" Alice Jordan ! Where then am I ? Or was it all
a terrible dream ? Is this Lovell Tower ? "

Alice's voice trembled as she said, " No."

" What then ? Oh ! I know now.   It is the Tower
of London, and the end cometh nigh."

" Nay, dearest mistress, you fare marvellous better
now."

" I mean not the fever-death, good friend, but
the end—the end of my weary pilgrimage, the gate
of the Happy City.   Welcome be the end of the way,
for the way hath been a rough one and a sore ! However
sharp be the end, I can bear it now.   My soul hath
been loosed from earth.   I see nothing now, I want
nothing but Christ, and to be with Him in the
glory.   Alice, how fareth the child ? I dared not to

ask afore, since I came into this place, but I can now."

"I trow he fareth well, good mistress, but of a long season I have not seen him. My Lord hath sent him unto the care of Dame Lovell."

Margery's eyes, rather than her voice, expressed her pleasure at this news.

"Hath my Lord my husband been here sithence I took sick ? "

"Every day, my Lady ; and I trow he sent away the boy for that reason, lest his coming hither should give him the sickness."

"Knoweth my mother of my sickness ? "

"I wis not, my Lady, but I trow that my Lord would tell her, when he sent the child down with Master Pynson."

"Master Pynson ! Hath he been hither ? "

"Yea, good my Lady, he came up, I ween, on Saint Luke's Day,[1] and took back the young master with him."

"What said he when ye told him of my prison, Alice ? "

"He covered his face, and wept sore."

Margery turned her face to the wall. "A fiery

[1] October 18.

trial!" she murmured, as if to herself—"a fiery trial for him as well as me! Is this the way wherein the Father will draw him? If so, Richard, I can bear it."

The 16th of February came. On the morning of that day, as Lord Marnell stepped out of his own house into the open air, with the intention of paying his usual visit to Margery, Abbot Bilson came up, radiant and smiling, and carrying under his arm a large parchment roll.

"Ah, my very good Lord, well met! Whither away?"

"I purpose to see Madge."

"Ah!" exclaimed the Abbot, who was occupied with an amusement which comes naturally to men of his disposition, and has been wittily defined as "washing one's hands with invisible soap, in imperceptible water."

"What hast under thine arm, reverend father?" asked Lord Marnell.

"Ah! this is the indictment of the Lady Marnell. Your Lordship witteth that she will be examined to-morrow afore the council, and by them sentenced."

"You will endeavour yourself, reverend father, that the sentence be made as light as may be."

"My Lord, we have but one sentence for heretics," said Abbot Bilson, with a smile which showed all his teeth, like a wild beast. "The Act regarding them was yestermorn sceptred by the King's Grace."

"One!" remarked Lord Marnell, in some surprise. "The sentence now, then, is—— ?"

"*Death.*"

Lord Marnell hastily laid his hand on a buttress, to steady himself, when he heard this awful news.

"You have deceived me, father! You have deceived me!" he cried. "You told me, some months gone, when first I called you into this matter, that the sentence on heretics was prison."

"My good Lord, I pray you remember that I told you but a moment back, that the new Act is just passed. Ere that the sentence truly was close prison ; but now—— "

On finding himself thus inveigled by the cunning of Abbot Bilson, Lord Marnell was beside himself with passion. He burst into a torrent of the most fearful language. Abbot Bilson stood calmly by, as if quite accustomed to such scenes.

"My good Lord, I pray you blaspheme not, or I must needs appoint you a sore penance," was all that he mildly observed.

Lord Marnell recovered himself by a strong effort, and asked, as politely as he could, what description of death was commanded by the new Act.

"Burning or beheading, at the pleasure of the King's Grace," replied the Abbot, as unconcernedly as though the choice in question lay between a couple of straws.

"My wife, being a peeress, will of force be beheaded?"

"Likely, I trow," replied the Abbot, drawing his cowl closer over his head, as a cold blast of wind came up the street.

"Father, you must use all effort that the sentence be so pronounced, if the King's Grace remit it not."

"The King's Grace remitteth never sentence on heretics," said Bilson, with another of his disagreeable smiles. "He is much too true and faithful son of Holy Church therefor. And as to my poor efforts, my Lord—— "

'You *can*, and you *shall*," wrathfully answered

Lord Marnell, and, not to prolong the contest, walked rapidly away.

Abbot Bilson stood looking after him, with an expression on his face not unlike that which a triumphant demon might be supposed to exhibit.

CHAPTER IX.

AN OBDURATE HERETIC.

" Great your strength, if great your need."
                                    —HENRY KIRKE WHITE.

IN the evening of the same day, the council sent a physician to report on the prisoner's health. Not gentle Master Simon, but a stern, iron-handed, iron-hearted man, from whom Margery and Alice shrank instinctively. The physician reported that the Lady Marnell had undoubtedly been very ill, but was now better, and ailed nothing but weakness ; he accordingly recommended that the examination should take place, but that the prisoner, in consideration of her extreme debility, should be indulged with a seat. Master Simon tried hard to obtain a little further postponement ; but this time the powerful Abbot was against him, and he gained nothing by his motion. So, on the morning of the 17th, Margery rose from her sick-bed to appear before the council.

Lord Marnell, who had lately shown her extraordinary kindness, as though with the view of undoing, so far as lay in his power, the evil which his rash, though well-meant conduct had originally created, assisted his wife into her litter, and rode beside it during the short journey. On arriving at the door, where they found a steep flight of steps to mount, Lord Marnell would not allow Margery to try her strength, but carried her up in his arms. He knew, and so did she, that she would need all the strength she could muster for the trial which was to come. The council-chamber was hung with red cloth, and the benches appropriated to spectators were filled to overflowing. For one moment Margery shrank back at the sight of so many strange faces; and a faint tinge of colour mounted to her pale cheek as Lord Marnell led her forward to her chair. In the president's seat was the Archbishop of Canterbury, and on his left hand Abbot Bilson. Several abbots, priors, and other legal and ecclesiastical dignitaries, made up the remainder of the council.

For eight weary hours, with very short intervals for refreshment, they kept that fragile prisoner before them, and all the time she never quailed, nor evaded any of their questions. Twice Master Simon interfered, and begged that wine might be given her, or he would not answer for her further recovery ; and once she herself asked for a glass of water, and for a few minutes seemed about to faint.

Abbot Bilson came out in his true colours at this examination. He was no longer the mild, persuasive teacher ; he now showed himself the unforgiving revenger. The Archbishop pressed the prisoner hard with questions, many of them irrevelant to the indictment ; and most of the other members of the Council put queries to her.

They inquired, amongst other things, if she believed that in the Sacrament of the Lord's Supper the bread and wine became the very body and blood of Christ.

"Nay, certes," was Margery's answer. "For if Christ, being in life, could hold His own body, and give the same unto His disciples, then were it no true human body, for a natural and true body cannot be in two several places at the self-same moment of time. Moreover, if the bread of the host be verily the body of Christ, then did He eat His own body, and that is contrary to very reason."

"The mysteries of the faith be above reason," said Arundel.

" Of a truth, and farther above it, maybe, than we wit ; but in no wise contrary thereunto."

" Believe you in Purgatory ? "

" The Church teacheth the same, and I say not that it may not be true ; but I find it not in the book."

" Pray you unto the blessed Virgin Saint Mary, the holy angels, and the saints ? "

" Soothly, no : it is not in the book. ' *Whateuer thing ye axen the Fadir in my name, I schal do that thing,*' saith Christ : but I hear not a word of ' whatever thing ye shall ask Saint Michael, or Saint Anne.' "

" Account you confession unto priests to be right or evil ? "

" It may be right—I wis not ; but I saw it not in the book. I pray you, reverend fathers, if any other part of God His book do name these things, and give leave for the same, that you show it unto me, and thereupon I will believe them, but no else."

The above is, of course, a mere sample of the innumerable questions which were put to the prisoner. Towards the close of the day, the Archbishop and abbots consulted together for a few minutes ; and then Arundel turned to the accused.

" Margery Marnell, Baroness Marnell of Lymington, the Court demands of you whether you will put your name to this paper, and hold to all things therein contained ? "

" Let me read the paper, my Lord Archbishop, and then I will give you an answer."

The Archbishop did not wish her to read the paper ; but Margery steadily declined to sign anything in the dark. At length the council permitted it to be read to her. It contained a promise to abjure all Lollard doctrines, and to perform a severe penance, such as the council should lay on her, for the scandal which she had caused to the Church. Margery at once refused to sign anything of the kind. The Archbishop warned her that in that case she must be prepared to submit to the capital sentence.

" Ye may sentence me," she said, in her clear voice, always distinct, however feeble, " to what ye will. I fear you not. I wis ye have power to kill my body, but my soul never shall ye have power to touch. That is Christ's, who witteth full well how to keep it ; and to His blessed hands, not yours, I commit myself, body and soul."

The Archbishop then passed sentence. The Court found Margery, Baroness Marnell of Lymington, guilty of all crimes whereof she stood indicted, and sentenced her to death by burning, in the open place called Tower Hill, on the 6th day of March next ensuing.

The prisoner bowed her head when the sentence had been pronounced, and then said as she rose, and stretched out her hand to Lord Marnell, who came forward and supported her, " I greatly fear, reverend fathers, that your day is yet to come, when you shall receive sentence from a Court whence there is no appeal, and shall be doomed to a dreader fire ! "

When Lord Marnell had assisted his wife back into her dungeon, and laid her gently on the bed, he turned and shook his fist at the wall.

" If I, Ralph Marnell of Lymington, had thee here, Abbot Thomas Bilson—— "

" Thou wouldst forgive him, my good Lord," faintly said Margery.

" Who ? I ? Forgive *him ?* What a woman art thou, Madge ! Nay—by the bones of Saint Matthew, I would break every bone in his body ! Forsooth, Madge, those knaves the Archbishop and the Abbot have played me a scurvy trick, and gone many times further than I looked for, when I called them into this business. But it is so always, as I have heard, —thy chirurgeon and thy confessor, if they once bear the hand in thy matters, will never let thee go till

they have choked thee. I fear I shall have hard
labour to get thee out of this scrape. I will do all
I can, be thou sure, but thou wist that I am not in
favour with the new King as I was with King Richard,
whose soul God rest! Madge, wilt forgive me,
wife?"

"With a very good will, my Lord," said Margery.
"I wis well that thou wottedst not all that thou didst."

"Not I, by Saint James of Compostella!" exclaimed
Lord Marnell. "Were the good King Richard alive
and reigning, I would soon let both the Archbishop
and the Abbot feel the place too hot for to hold them.
But I can do nothing with Harry of Bolingbroke,
looking, too, that he hateth the Lollards as he hateth
the devil—and a deal more, I trow, for I count that
that prince and he be old friends," added Lord Marnell,
with an air of great disgust.

Margery smiled gravely. She felt sorry for her
husband, who she saw was very miserable himself
at the unexpected result of his conduct; but she did
not allow herself for an instant to hope that he could
save her.

"Mine own good Lord," she said, "I pray you
torment not yourself in assaying my relief, neither
in thinking that you be the cause of my trouble;

for I forgive you as freely as Christ hath forgiven me, and I count that is free enough."

Lord Marnell stood leaning against the wall, and looking at Margery, who lay outside the bed.

"Of a truth, wife, I conceive thee not. Thou art here in the Tower dungeon, and thou lookest for no good outcoming, and lo! thou art calm and peaceful as if thou wert on King Henry's throne! What means it, Madge?"

"I trow I am much happier here than I should be on King Henry's throne!" answered Margery, with a smile. "Christ is with me, good husband, and where Christ is, is peace. '*Pees I leeue to ghou, my pees I ghyue to ghou; not as the world ghyueth I ghyue to ghou.*'[1] '*These thingis I haue spoken to ghou, that ghe haue pees in me. In the world ghe schulen haue disese; but triste ghe, I haue ouercome the world.*'"[2]

When Lord Marnell quitted Margery that evening, he hastened to Court, and attempted to gain the ear of the King. Since the deposition of his friend and master, King Richard, he had never appeared there. He was consequently a stranger to the pages and porters, who tried to get rid of him as politely as they could. At length Lord Marnell caught sight of

[1] John xiv. 27.   [2] John xvi. 33.

the Earl of Surrey, who with some hesitation consented to introduce him into the privy chamber. Henry listened to Lord Marnell only until he comprehended the nature of his plea ; then met him with a frown and an angry—

" Pardon a Lollard ? Never ! "

" Please it, your Grace, your noble predecessor, King Richard, though no Lollard, would have granted me at once, in consideration of my long and faithful service unto him."

" I am not Richard of Bordeaux, but Henry of Bolingbroke ! " was the haughty answer, as the King turned round abruptly, and quitted Lord Marnell.

" By our Lady of Walsingham, I wis full well *that*," replied the latter, *sotto voce*.

As Lord Marnell quitted the palace, he met in the corridor with the Prince of Wales,[1] who stopped and saluted him, and Lord Marnell at once begged for his intercession with his father. The Prince readily promised it, but on learning particulars, the son's brow darkened as the father's had done. He was very sorry, but he really could not ask the King's pardon for a Lollard. Lord Marnell would have given his whole fortune to undo his own work of the

[1] Afterwards Henry V.

last eighteen months. He had never dreamed that Abbot Bilson would have summoned the archbishop to his aid, nor that Margery would have stood half as firmly as she had done. He only knew her as a fragile, gentle, submissive girl, and never expected to find in her material for the heroine or the martyr. Lord Marnell tried to procure the mediation of everybody about the Court ; but all, while expressing great sympathy with him, declined to risk their own necks. Even the King's sons said they dared not comply with his request. Prince Thomas [1] was extremely kind—very much grieved that he could not help him ; but Prince Humphrey [2] turned scornfully from him, and Prince John [3] coldly bade him take heed to his own safety. The Earl of Somerset, the King's halfbrother, shook his head, and said he was already suspected by the King to be a Lollard himself, and such an application from him would probably seal his own doom. Lord Marnell applied to the Queen ; [4] but she seemed most afraid of all to whom he had spoken, lest she should incur the King's anger, and possibly endanger herself.

The interval between the day of the examination

[1] Duke of Clarence. [2] Duke of Gloucester.
[3] The great Duke of Bedford.
[4] Jeanne of Navarre, the second wife of Henry IV.

and that appointed for the execution passed drearily
to all parties. Lord Marnell, notwithstanding all
these repulses, exerted himself unremittingly to procure
a commutation of the sentence, at least to beheading ;
but in vain. The King was inexorable. If the Lady
Marnell had chosen to ally herself with Lollards, she
well knew what she was doing, and must abide the
consequences. Vainly did Lord Marnell represent
how young and inexperienced she was ; in vain did
he urge that the Act which made the Lollards amenable
to capital punishment had been passed since her
indictment, and only a few weeks before. Henry
was not naturally disposed to hear his pleasure called
in question ; and Abbot Bilson had had possession
of the royal ear already.

When Alice returned from Marnell Place on the
evening of the 26th of February, Margery saw, by
the expression of her face, that she had heard something which shocked her. She asked what it was.

" You mind, good my Lady, the day that you
went with Master Pynson to hear a sermon in Bostock
Church ? "

" I trow I shall not lightly forget it," was Margery's
answer.

" Master Sastre was a-preaching, was he not ? "

" Aye. Wherefore ? "

" My Lady, he suffered death this forenoon by burning."

" Master Sastre ! Who told thee ? "

" Christopher it was that told me,—and yon evil man—for sure, though he be a holy priest, yet is he an evil man, or would he never else have so dealt with your Ladyship—yon evil man, Abbot Bilson was there, and did sore press Master Sastre for to have confessed his error ; but Master Sastre did maintain the same to the end."

Margery turned away her head. The venerable image of Sastre rose up before her, as he learned forward over the pulpit to say those last earnest words.

" Ah, dear old teacher ! " she whispered to herself. " Thou wilt not have long to look among the multitude in the white apparel, for *one* face which was upturned to thee that day ! "

CHAPTER X.

GLORIFYING THE LORD IN THE FIRES.

" Ah, little is all loss,
And brief the space 'twixt shore and shore,
If Thou, Lord Jesus, on us lay,
Through the dark waters of our way,
The burden which Christopheros bore—
To carry Thee across."
—MISS MULOCH.

AS Lord Marnell sat with Margery in her cell in the evening of the 1st of March, she begged him to grant her a favour. Her contrite husband bade her ask what she would. Margery replied that she greatly wished to write a last letter to her mother. Writing materials were carefully kept from her. Could Lord Marnell supply her with the means of doing so ? He said he would attempt it.

When Alice returned on the following day from Marnell Place, whither she had been to procure a change of linen for her mistress, she brought with her also a loaf of bread. The jailer demurred at this, but Alice urged that Lady Marnell did not like the bread made by the prison baker, and surely the jailer would not grudge her a loaf from home, for the few days she had to live. The jailer shook his head, but let it pass. When Alice was safe in the cell, she broke the loaf, and produced from it, cunningly imbedded in the soft crumb, several sheets of paper folded surprisingly small, a pen, and a little inkhorn. Margery's eyes glistened when she saw these, and she wrote her letter secretly during the night. But how to get it out of the prison with safety ? Alice was able to provide for this also. The letter was sewn in one of the pillows, which would be carried back to Marnell Place after the execution.

The last day of Lady Marnell's life sped away as other less eventful days do, and the evening of the 5th of March arrived. Alice, having just returned from her usual journey to the house, was disposing of the articles which she had brought with her, when the jailer's key grated in the lock, and the door was opened. Lady Marnell looked up, expecting to see her husband, though it was rather before his usual time for visiting her ; but on looking up, she saw Abbot Bilson.

This feline ecclesiastic came forward with bent head and joined hands, vouchsafing no reply to Margery's salutation of " Good even, father," nor to Alice's humble request for his blessing. He sat down on a chair, and for some minutes stared at Margery in silence—conduct so strange that at length she said, " Wherefore come you, father ? "

" To look at thee, child of the devil ! " was the civil answer.

Alice, who had just requested the blessing of the *priest,* was more angry than she could bear with the *man.* She was just on the point of saying something sharp, when Lord Marnell's voice behind the Abbot interposed with—

" If thou wouldst see a child of the devil, I trow thou hast little need to look further than thy mirror ! "

The Abbot rose calmly, and let Lord Marnell enter.

" It becometh not poor and humble monks, servitors of God, to lend themselves unto the vanity of mirrors," said he, pulling out a large rosary, and beginning to tell his beads devoutly.

" ' Servitors of God ! ' " cried Lord Marnell, too angry to be prudent. " Dost call thyself a servitor of God ? If God hath no better servitors than thou, I ween He is evil served ! "

The Abbot cast a glance from the corner of his eye at Lord Marnell, but made no answer, save to tell his beads more devoutly than ever.

" Hast no other place to tell thy beads in ? " asked that nobleman.

The Abbot rose without a word, and, pausing at the door, stretched his hand over the assembled trio, and muttered some words to himself.

" Away with thee, Lucifer, and thy maledictions ! " exclaimed Lord Marnell. " There be here who are nearer to the angels than ever thou shalt be ! "

Suddenly the Abbot was gone. Nobody had seen or heard him depart—he seemed to melt into the night, in some strange, mysterious way.

" He is gone, and Satan his master go with him ! " said Lord Marnell. " Ho, jailer ! lock the door, I pray, and leave us three alone together."

The jailer obeyed ; and Lord Marnell sat down by the side of Margery's bed, and bade Alice lie down on her own pallet, and sleep if she could. He gave the same counsel to Margery ; but the latter smiled, and said she would never sleep again in this world.

" Now, Madge ! " said her husband, " hast aught on thy mind, good wife, that thou wouldst say ere morn ? Aught that I can do for thee ? Trust me, I will do the same right gladly."

Margery thanked him fervently ; there was a heartiness in his tone which was not often audible.

"There be a few matters, mine own good Lord, which under thy good pleasure I would willingly have done. I would that all my servants might have a year's pay; and for Alice, poor lass! who hath tended me so well and truly, I pray that a small matter of money may be given her by the year: moreover, I would like, if she will—for I would not lay her under bond—that she should keep with Geoffrey while she liveth, or at least until he be a man. And, good husband, I would that thou wouldst teach my poor child to remember me, his mother, but above all, to remember the Lord for whom I die, and who, having loved me in the world, loveth me unto the end.[1] Tell him to count nought too good for Christ. I trust Christ hath set His heart upon him—I have prayed for him too much else— and He promised me that whatever thing I should ask the Father in His name He would do that thing." [2]

"Hast thou prayed ever for me, good wife?" asked Lord Marnell.

"Many times, my good Lord, and I will do so till I die."

"The Church teacheth that dying stoppeth not praying," said he.

[1] John xiii. 1.   [2] John xvi. 16.

" I wis well that the Church so teacheth ; but I saw it not in the book ; however, if I find it to be so, I will pray God for thee there also."

" Thou sayest well, Madge ; but I trow thou art more angel presently than shall I be ever. I tell thee, Madge—for mayhap it will comfort thee to know it—thy dealings and sayings of late have caused me to think more on these things than ever did I afore. It seemeth but a small matter to thee, to go through the fire to the glory. I marvel an' it could be so unto me."

" Say not ' to the glory,' good husband, but to Christ. I would not have the glory and lack Christ. And for thee, I do rejoice and bless God heartily, if He will make my poor doings of any good service unto the welfare of thy soul. And believe me, that if thou art called unto my fiery ordeal, Christ will give thee grace and strength equal unto thy need. It is not much for them who love Christ, if they see Him stand beyond a little fire, to pluck up heart and go through the fire to Him. O good husband, take these as my dying words, and teach them to the child for the same, ' Christ without everything is an hundredfold better than everything without Christ ! ' "

Those last words were ringing in Lord Marnell's

ears when, about eight o'clock in the morning, he
stood on the steps of Marnell Place, looking towards
the Tower, and fancying the mournful preparations
which were going on there. Margery had thought
it best that she should be alone for her fiery trial.
As Lord Marnell stood there, lost in thought, he
suddenly heard his own name spoken. He turned
round, and saw two men before him, in travellers'
attire. One of them was an old man, with venerable
white head and beard ; the other was much younger,
and Lord Marnell recognised him at once.

"Master Pynson! I pray you what brings you
here ? Is the boy well ? "

"He is well," answered Richard, in a low tone,
"and Dame Lovell likewise. We came hither on
matters pertaining to my friend who here standeth,
and a terrible bruit hath reached us that the Lady
Marnell will suffer this morrow."

"It is true," said Lord Marnell, sorrowfully.

"Can no help be found ? " cried Richard, in an
agony. "I would put my life for hers—yea, an
hundred times twice told ! "

"And I likewise," said her husband. "No—there
is no help. The King will hear of no remittance."

"When is it ? "

"At nine o' the clock. You will come into the house and eat ?

Richard declined. He had already secured a chamber at the "Blue Boar," and would not trouble his Lordship.

"Come, Master Carew," said he to his companion, "let us be on our way."

"Go ye for to see her ?" inquired Lord Marnell.

"I will not lose sight of her," answered Richard, "until she be in the Paradise of God!"

Long before nine o'clock on the morning of that 6th of March, a large crowd was already gathered on Tower Hill. Some came there from a feeling of revenge—glad to see a Lollard burned. Among these was Archbishop Arundel. Some, from a feeling of deep pity for the poor young girl who was to be almost the protomartyr of the new faith. Among these were Pynson and Carew. The chief part of the concourse, however, shared neither of these feelings to any great degree, but came simply to see a sight, just as they would have gone to see a royal procession, or any other pageant.

As nine o'clock struck on the great bell of the Tower, the martyr appeared, led forth between the sheriff and Abbot Bilson. She was clothed in one long white garment, falling from her throat to her feet; and, notwithstanding the inclemency of the weather, her head, arms, and feet were bare. No fastening confined her golden hair, which streamed freely over her shoulders and fell around her. She walked slowly, but quite calmly. Arrived at the place of execution, the sheriff urged her to confess.

"I will confess," said Margery, "to Him who can alone absolve me." And lifting up her eyes, she said, "O Lord God, who art above all things, and hast given Thy Son to die for us sely and sinful men, I confess to Thee that I am a vile sinner, utterly unworthy of Thy grace and mercy. That day by day, for twenty-three years, have I done what I ought not, and said what I ought not, and thought what I ought not. That all my life also have I left undone things the which I ought for to have done. Wherefore, O Father, let it please Thee of Thy goodness to forgive me, and to look not on me, but on Thy Son Christ, in whose rightwiseness I am rightwise, and who hath loved me as Thou hast loved also Him. O Lord God, turn not away the face of Thy servant, whose heart Thou hast moved to pray thus unto Thee!"

The Abbot and the sheriff were extremely annoyed,

but they did not dare to silence her, for the multitude hung breathlessly on her words.

"There's none so much harm in *that*, any way!" said a woman who stood near Richard Pynson.

"Wilt thou confess, sinful heretic?" asked the Abbot.

"To God I will and have done," answered Margery; "to man I will not."

There was a short pause, while the sheriff's men, under his direction, heaped the wood in the position most favourable for burning quickly. Then the sheriff read the indictment in a loud voice. It was a long document, and took upwards of twenty minutes to read. After this, they passed a chain round Margery's body, and fastened her to the stake. The sheriff then, with a lighted torch, advanced to set the wood on fire.

"Will ye allow me that I may speak unto the people?" asked Margery of the Abbot.

"No, miserable reprobate!" said he, "thou hast spoken too much already!"

"I pray Christ forgive you all that you have done unto me!" was the martyr's answer.

The sheriff now applied the torch. Meanwhile Margery stood on the pile of wood, with her hands clasped on her bosom, and her eyes lifted up to heaven. What means it? Does she feel no pain? How is it that, as the flames spring up and roar around her, there is no tremor of the clasped hands, no change in the rapturous expression of the white upturned face? And from the very midst of those flames comes a voice, the silver voice of Margery Lovell, as clear and melodious as if she stood quietly in the hall at Lovell Tower—

"*Worthy is the Lamb that was slain to take virtue, and Godhead, and wisdom, and strength, and honour, and glory*——"

But the voice fails there, and the "blessing" is spoken to the angels of God.

And from the outskirts of the crowd comes another voice which is very like the voice of Richard Pynson—

"*I am agen risyng and lyf; he that beleeueth in me, yhe though he be deed, he schal lyue; and ech that lyueth and bileueth into me, schal not dye withouten eende.*" [1]

"The noble army of martyrs praise Thee," softly adds old Carew.

Thus did Margery Marnell glorify the Lord in the fires.

[1] John xi. 25.

CHAPTER XI.

MARGERY'S LETTER.

"So that day there was dole in Astolat."
—TENNYSON.

THE winter had just given place to spring, and a bright, fresh morning rose on Lovell Tower. Dame Lovell was busy in the kitchen, as she was when we first saw her, and so were Mistress Katherine and the handmaidens; but Dame Lovell now wore the white weeds of widowhood, and her face was thinner and much graver. Richard Pynson, on his return from London, had brought her the terrible news of Margery's death; and Dame Lovell, in the midst of her sorrow, which was very deep, had solemnly affirmed that no power on earth should ever induce her to pardon her son-in-law for the part which he had taken in the matter.

Richard Pynson, long before this, had mooted the question of his return to his father, but Dame Lovell would not hear of it. He reminded her smilingly that *she* needed no squire; but she came and put both her hands on his shoulders, and made him look her in the face.

"Thou sayest sooth, Richard, that I need no squire, but I trow I need a son. I am an old lone woman, and shall not keep thee long; and I have loved thee as if I had been thine own mother. Promise me, mine own dear lad, that thou wilt not go hence while I live."

Richard looked up with the tears in his eyes, and told her, as he kissed her hand, that it was no wish of his to depart, and that he would not do so without her full consent.

"That shalt thou have never!" was the answer.

So Richard remained at Lovell Tower. On the morning of which I speak, little Geoffrey, who was very fond of Richard, and was petted by him perhaps rather more than was good for him, had suddenly espied him at the farther end of the garden, and instantly rushed after him as fast as his little legs would carry him. A few minutes afterwards, Cicely came into the kitchen from the hall, and announced to her mistress that a strange gentleman wished to see her. Dame Lovell took off her apron, and rinsed her hands in water.

"See thou to the marchpane, Kat," remarked she to Mistress Katherine, as she went to receive her guest.

It was no wonder that Cicely had not known him, for some seconds elapsed before Dame Lovell herself could recognise Lord Marnell. Six years had passed since they met at his marriage to Margery, but he looked at least twenty years older. His figure was still upright, though much thinner, but the very form of his features seemed changed, and his rich auburn hair was now white as drifted snow. His manner, which had been blunt and almost boisterous, was remarkably quiet. When he saw that Dame Lovell did not recognise him, he said, with a smile—

"You know me not, fair mother?"

Dame Lovell's astonishment overcame her enmity for the moment.

"Troth, I knew thee not, good son! is it truly thou? Nay, how changed art thou!"

"I wis that well," he answered. "Where is Geoffrey?"

"I trow he be in the garden with Richard," replied Dame Lovell. "I will bid him hither."

Little Geoffrey, holding Richard's hand, as if he would not part with him for a moment, returned to the house at his grandmother's bidding ; but like her, he could not recognise his father, whom he had not seen for some months, until Lord Marnell's well-known voice assured him of his identity. He rather shrank from him, as usual ; but when Lord Marnell contrary to his custom, lifted him up and kissed him, he seemed a little reassured, and sat on his father's knee, staring at him intently. Lord Marnell gave a cordial greeting to Richard, and then, observing how earnestly his little son's eyes were fixed upon him, asked him at what he was looking.

"What have you done with your hair ? " was Master Geoffrey's puzzled answer.

Lord Marnell laughed, and told the child that everybody's hair turned white as they grew old.

"But your Lordship's hath done so quickly," remarked Richard.

"That were no great marvel," he answered, gravely.

Dame Lovell found it rather difficult to keep up her revengeful determination. She was naturally a very easy-tempered woman, and the evident change, moral as well as physical, in Lord Marnell, touched her, and melted her enmity considerably.

"I pray you, fair mother," he said, looking up, " to leave me tell you wherefore I came hither. Firstly,

it was to give you a letter from Madge, which she
wrote in the Tower unto you." And Lord Marnell,
passing his hand into his breast, pulled out a small
square packet, tied with blue silk, and sealed with
yellow wax. It was directed—

"*To the hands of my singular good lady and most
dear mother, Dame Agnes Lovell, at Lovell Tower, be
these delivered with speed.*"

Dame Lovell kissed the letter, and placed it in her
own bosom. She could not read a word of it, but
it was enough that it came from Margery.

"Secondarily," pursued Lord Marnell, "I would
fain ask you, fair mother, for to keep Geoffrey here
a while longer, for I wis not yet what I shall do."

"That will I, right heartily," said Dame Lovell,
in a tone as cordial as her words.

"Moreover, an' it stand with your pleasure, I
would pray you for to take back Alice Jordan, as you
will find in yon letter that Madge did desire her for
to be about Geoffrey, if she would, and she seemeth
right fain."

"I will have her with a very good will," answered
Dame Lovell, "and she shall be next in mine house
unto Mistress Katherine, and shall eat at the high
table."

Lord Marnell thanked her sincerely for her readiness to comply with his wishes. He said that Alice should come down to Lovell Tower as soon as she could conveniently set out, and old Christopher, as the most trusty of his household, should escort her. There was silence for a short time, and then, with a kind of shadow of a smile, Lord Marnell said suddenly—

"Do you hate me, fair mother?"

"I did afore I saw thee this morrow," replied Dame Lovell, candidly.

"And wherefore not after?"

"Meseemeth thou hast repented thyself of thy deed."

"Repented!" said Lord Marnell, mournfully. "Mother, will you crede me if I tell you that no sorrow worser than this can ever befall me, and that had I known what would come of my seeking of Abbot Bilson, I had sooner cut off my right hand?"

"I do," said she.

"Madge knew it, poor damsel! and she said she forgave me in such manner as Christ did forgive herself. Will you do the like, mother?"

"With all mine heart and soul, good son!" cried Dame Lovell, every shred of her animosity vanished, and the tears fairly running down her cheeks.

"Don't cry, g'ammer!" exclaimed little Geoffrey, jumping off his father's knee and running to Dame Lovell. "What are you crying for? Somebody hurt you? If they have, I'll kill 'em!"

Dame Lovell laughed through her tears at Master Geoffrey's threat. She was a good deal surprised when Lord Marnell spoke of going away; but he said he had promised his cousin Sir Ralph that he would stay with him next time he came into the neighbourhood; and he must return to London in a day or two. So he only remained to dinner, and departed immediately afterwards, evoking from Geoffrey the significant remark that "he liked him a great deal better this time."

That evening, Dame Lovell and Friar Andrew sat down by the fire to listen to that last letter. Her widow's dress, somewhat resembling that of a nun, but pure white, left only her eyes, nose, and mouth visible. Richard Pynson, in a rather more ambitious costume than the page's suit wherein we made his acquaintance, seated himself in the opposite corner. How like Margery's voice the letter sounded, in that old hall at Lovell Tower!—so much so, that it seemed scarcely a stretch of fancy to expect her to glide down the stair which led from her chamber, where her child now lay sleeping. How well Richard could recall the scene when, six years before, she came softly down to receive from his hand the cherished and fatal volume !

Richard broke the seal, while Friar Andrew threw back his cowl, and Dame Lovell smoothed her apron, and bent forward to listen.

"MINE OWN DEAR MOTHER,—In as humble and lowly manner as I may, I commend myself unto you, praying you of your daily blessing.

"Whereas I hear that Richard Pynson hath been here in London on St. Luke's Day last, and hath borne back Geoffrey with him, at the which news I am truly glad, I trow that you have heard of my close prison in the Tower, whence I now write. I pray you therefore, good mother, not to lay this overmuch to heart, neither to grieve for me ; for I certify unto you that never was I so happy and blessed as now I am, when over the dark water, which is death, I can see a glimpse of the Happy City. Neither, good mother, be downcast, I beseech you, when you shall hear that on Sunday, the eve of Saint Anselm, I am to die. I pray you, dear mother, if you knew that on Sunday I should be advanced to some high

place in the Court, would you sorrow ? Yea, would
you not rejoice greatly therefor ? Wherefore I entreat
you, sorrow not now, but rejoice rather, for I am to
be taken up into an high place, yea, passing high—
even the Court of Christ Himself, whence also none of
those changes and evils can cast me down again,
which are ever coming upon them who live in this
world.

"Moreover, good mother, I do you to wit that
this is Christ's truth for the which I suffer, and that
Christ Himself is with me. Yea, I think on Christ
as He that is standing on the other side of the fire ;
and shall I not then make haste through the same
that I may come at Him ?

"Likewise I do beseech you, mine own dear mother,
grieve not when you think that I have had but little
joy or gladness in this my short life. If divers children
be playing in a garden, and the serving-man do come
and fetch away some afore others, that they may see
their elders, and may have brave gifts the which be
ready for them at home, fall they a-weeping, think
you, because they must lose an hour of play ? Nay,
truly not, if their hearts be set on the brave gifts afore
them. So, good mother, though you have passed in
this weary and evil life nigh sixty years, and I only

twenty-three, count it, I beseech you, but an hour more or less of child's playing, which will surely be made up to us when we go home, and receive the brave gifts which our Father hath for us in His storehouse. And if I have not known joy as much as some, I have the less for to leave behind me in the case wherein I now am. For you know, good mother, that at the first I was wedded against mine own will and liking ; and though I may and must say unto you for my Lord my husband, that in this evil case he hath been more gentler unto me than ever afore, and hath drawn mine heart much closer unto him, yet nathless I may say also that an' I had been with mine own will wedded, I trow that I had had far more for to leave for Christ, and had found far more hardship in the doing of it. For God doeth all His work well ; and He wist surely what He did when my dear father—whose soul God rest !—was let wed me thus.

" Behold now, most dear mother, how I have taken from you all cause of your lamentation, and have left you nothing but to rejoice for me ! Wherefore rejoice for me, for at this time a sennight hence, I shall be singing with the angels of God. I trow that one look at Christ Jesu will pay me all mine account in the

small matter I have suffered for Him. I trow that
if He but smile, and say, 'Thou art welcome, dear
child, for I have loved thee,' I shall count the fires of
this world but light gear then. Will you sorrow that
I am in good case? Will you grieve because I am
blessed? Will you count you have lost your child,
when she is singing in the great glory? Nay, good
mother, I wis I have well said in praying you to rejoice
rather.

"And, dear mother, I beseech you that you bring
up mine own dear child in the same. I would have
him, if I may, as dear unto Christ as I am, and as
ready to leave all for Christ His sake, as I, his mother,
have done. I say not this, God witteth, to magnify
my poor deeds, the which I know well be vile enough
and want as much and great washing in Christ His
blood, as the worst sin that ever I did,—but, good
mother, teach my boy of Christ! Count it not anything that he leaveth for Him. Yea, forsooth, rather
would I a thousandfold that he should live on a dry
crust for Christ, than that he should have many
brave dishes and rich fare without Him. To this
end I beseech you, most dear mother, that you will
have the child learned for to read, and will get that
he may read God's Word, which hath shown me how

dear and gracious is Christ Jesus. I pray you spare no pains ne goods for to do this.

" Dear mother, I have prayed my Lord my husband that, if she will, Alice Jordan shall have the care of Geoffrey. She hath been a good and true serving-woman unto me, and she witteth how I would have him ordered. I pray you, therefore, if she come unto you, that you would put her about him. Like-wise commend me, I beseech you, unto mine ancient friends and fellows, and all the meynie, and bid them learn for to love Christ Jesu, and we shall then meet shortly again. Specially I would desire mine humble service unto dear Father Andrew, and I do beg him for my sake to read for himself the blessed book which hath been my comfort.

" And to end,—for I will weary you no longer, dear friend Richard Pynson, with reading of mine evil hand, and I give you God's blessing and mine for the kindness you have done unto me, and pray you not to forget the last words which I said unto you with my voice, but to keep fast hold of Christ, till you know and love Him better than any friend in this evil world,—so to end, dear mother, I beseech you that you would forgive me all wherein I have been an ill daughter unto you, and all things wherein at any time I have troubled you. Good mother, I am happy. I am looking out of the night to see the day-dawn breaking. Come Sunday, I shall be in heaven. Come Sunday, by God's mercy—not by mine own good, which God witteth is but evil—I shall stand with the angels before Christ His throne. Haste, haste, dear good day that shall deliver me! And God give you to know Christ, and send us a happy meeting in that His blessed habitation, unto the great gladding of your most loving and dutiful daughter, MARGERY MARNELL.

"Written this second of March, from the gate of the *Urbs Beata*."

CHAPTER XII.

EASTWARD HO!

"Whether he go to East or West,
With Christ he always is at home."
—NEWTON.

FOR a few minutes after Richard finished reading the letter, there was silence, unbroken save by the sound of weeping, in the old hall. Friar Andrew cried like a child. Dame Lovell, too, wept profusely, especially at the passage in which Margery begged her forgiveness, and sobbed forth that she had nothing to forgive her. Richard had hard work to read. He heard her voice in every line, and when he came to the one sentence addressed to himself, he very nearly broke down altogether. After that long pause, Richard, who had been sitting with his head buried in his hands, looked up and spoke.

"Mistress, you mind that I did promise you not to go hence save with your good will?"

164

" Well, Richard ? "

" May I have the same, good mistress, for a season ? "

" Where wouldst go, lad ? Dost want to see thy father ? I meant not to let [1] thee from going home at times, so thou leave me not wholly."

" You do misconceive me, mistress. I trust soothly, to go but for a season, though mayhap a long one ; but not home. An' you will give me leave, and I have my father's goodwill to it, I shall go abroad."

" Go *where*, Richard ? " asked Dame Lovell, in some alarm and no little astonishment.

" Anywhere," he answered, listlessly, " that is far enough away. I shall wend unto the East Country."

" Eh, Richard ! thou wilt be slain of robbers ! " cried Friar Andrew. " All yon country is full filled of Saracens and heathens, who think no more of shedding Christian blood than of cooking a capon."

" I shall be slain, good father, I trow, if I stay here. There is no peace heraway in England for them who read God's Word, and I have read it. I should quickly be indicted, I ween, for a Lollard, an'

---

[1] Hinder. The modern signification of this word is exactly the opposite of its original meaning.

I stayed. Master Carew told me yestre'en, that there were spies hereabouts, and he did trow he was suspected. And if they take him, they will come next to me."

" Richard ! Richard ! " cried Dame Lovell. " Thou frightest me, lad ! But wilt thou go, soothly ? I wis not how to leave thee do so."

" Dear mistress," said Richard, in a low tone, " I pray God and you to pardon me, but I fear I am only a poor caitiff coward. I could not bear the fiery ordeal which Margery has borne. I will confess to you, good lady, that night and day I do pray God to spare me the same. I had better go, ere I am tired, and perchance fail and deny my Master. I will give you to wit of my welfare, in case I should meet any Palmers on their way home, and may be I can come back, an' there should rise a king who shall give us leave to live."

" Well, my lad ! I trow I must not let thee ! " said Dame Lovell, in a grieved tone. " I wis not how to do without thee, Richard ; but I ween I should sorrow more to keep thee and bring thee to grief, than in leaving thee go away from me."

The following day brought a servant in Lord Marnell's livery, with a letter to Richard.

"*To the hands of Master Richard Pynson, at Lovell Tower, give these.*

"GOOD MASTER PYNSON,—I pray you for to look warily unto your ways ; for I hear by messengers from London that you be suspected for a Lollard, and Abbot Bilson hath your name on his list of evil affected unto the Church. If you can wend for a time unto some other country, I trow you would find your safety in so doing. I beseech you burn this letter, or it may do me a mischief.

"It hath come into my mind that Madge did name unto me your desire of knighthood. If such be still your wish, I pray you make use of me in this matter. Let me wit by the bearer of these your pleasure herein, and if you desire to watch this even, I will meet you in Bostock Church early on the morrow.

"I set out on my way to London to-morrow.

"Commend me in all lowly fashion to my good mother ; and with God's blessing and mine to the child, I rest, your loving friend,   R. MARNELL."

Richard read Lord Marnell's letter to Dame Lovell, and then at once put it in the fire. He determined to accept the kind offer thus made to him ; and accordingly he sent word by the messenger that he would be ready to meet Lord Marnell in Bostock Church, at any early hour on the following morning.

Knighthood was then conferred in two ways. A knight-banneret was one created on the field of battle. An ordinary knight was required to be of good family and of a suitable age, and the accolade was given him after a night's fasting and watching in some church. Other, but less important ceremonies were also observed. This latter course was necessarily the one chosen by Richard. At five o'clock on the following morning, Lord Marnell met him in Bostock Church, and gave him the stroke on the shoulder with the flat of his sword, which was required to make its recipient a knight. [1] Richard thanked Lord Marnell fervently for his warning, and also for his kindness in offering him knighthood ; and told him that he had already

---

[1] Knighthood is now conferred only by the Sovereign, who is "the fountain of honour," or by a viceroy, as representing the Sovereign. In ancient times, however, "a knight could make a knight." When the Duke of Suffolk was taken prisoner in battle by a simple squire, he asked, before surrendering his sword, "Are you a knight ?" "No," was the answer. "Kneel, then," replied Suffolk, "that I may make you one ; for I will never give up my sword to a squire." The squire knelt, and Suffolk knighted his captor, and then delivered his sword to one who, by the laws of chivalry, had now become his equal.

resolved to go abroad, before receiving his letter.

" I think you will do well," said he ; " but I pray you, Sir Richard, to lose no time, for spies be about in Marston even now."

Late that night, after an affectionate farewell to Dame Lovell and Friar Andrew, and a warm kiss to little Geoffrey, who was fast asleep, Sir Richard Pynson set out on his long and perilous journey. Dame Lovell sent with him one of her own servants, a man who she knew would imperil his own life sooner than that of Richard ; and he returned to her in a few days with the welcome tidings that he had seen Richard safely embarked on a vessel for La Rochelle, with Master Carew's son, a youth of about eighteen, as his squire. The servant had, however, more, and less agreeable news than this to tell ; for as he passed through Marston, he had been told that Master Carew was arrested, and on his journey to London under a strong guard.

So set in the bitter persecution, which was to last for many weary years.

A full twelvemonth had passed since Richard's departure. Of Lord Marnell, Dame Lovell had neither seen nor heard anything more. Alice Jordan had

arrived, to little Geoffrey's great delight; but she
had only been able to report the return of her master
to London, as she had left that place the day after
his arrival. Dame Lovell fulfilled her promise of
promotion for Margery's humble but faithful friend,
who was henceforth generally addressed in the house
as "Mistress" Alice. Little Geoffrey, though somewhat consoled by Alice's appearance, missed Richard
sorely; and demanded of his grandmother at least
once a day, "when he would come back?"

The family and household were seated at supper,
on a summer afternoon in the year 1402, when the
sound of a horn outside the moat sent one of the
farm-servants hurriedly to the gate. He returned
saying, "A holy Palmer, good mistress, seeketh
entrance."

"A Palmer! bring him in speedily, good Hodge!"
exclaimed Dame Lovell. "Blessed is the house
whereinto entereth a Palmer,—and mayhap he may
give us to wit of Richard."

The Palmer was attired in a long coat of coarse
brown frieze, with a large flapped hat, not unlike that
of a coal-heaver. He was conducted to the high
table, where Friar Andrew served him with meat,
and put all manner of questions to him. He had

come, he said, from Damascus, where he had met with a friend of theirs, one Sir Richard Pynson, and he brought a packet from him ; which he thereupon took from his wallet, and delivered into Dame Lovell's hands.   It was a large packet, and evidently contained something more than merely a letter.   Dame Lovell was highly delighted, particularly when, on opening the parcel, she drew out a magnificent piece of baudekyn, one of the richest dress-stuffs then made, and only to be procured from Constantinople.   Beside this the packet only contained a letter, which Dame Lovell was sorely puzzled how to read.   There was nobody at Lovell Tower who could read except Friar Andrew, and he, as has been previously stated, was not by any means a first-class scholar.   However, Dame Lovell passed him the letter, and after spending some time in the examination of it, he announced that he thought he could read it, " for the lad had written the letters great, like a good lad, as he always was." Richard had, indeed, purposely done so, because he anticipated that Friar Andrew would have to read it. The Palmer interposed, saying that he could read well, and offered to read the letter ; but this Dame Lovell civilly declined, because she thought there might be secrets in the letter, and she did not know whether the Palmer were to be trusted. Friar Andrew was mechanically retiring into one of the deep windows, but Dame Lovell stopped him, and requested him to follow her to her own room. She gathered up her baudekyn, and left the servants to entertain the Palmer, who she gave orders should be feasted with the best in the house.

"Now, father," said Dame Lovell, when she had Friar Andrew and the letter safe in her own apartment, "Now read, I pray thee; but we will have no eavesdroppers, and though Palmers be holy men, yet may they carry tales."

Friar Andrew sat down, cleared his throat, and began to read rather grandiloquently. He read syllable by syllable, like a child, and every now and then stumbled over a hard word. As to the names of places, he declared himself unable to read those at all. I therefore purpose to give the letter, not as Andrew read it, but as Richard wrote it.

"*To the hands of the very worthy Dame, my good lady and mistress, Dame Agnes Lovell, of Lovell Tower, be these delivered with all convenient speed.*

"DEAR MISTRESS AND MY WORTHY DAME,—In as humble and lowly wise as may be, I commend myself to your kindly favour, hoping that these may find you in health, as they leave me presently. I do you to wit, good mistress, that I have arrived safely, by the grace of our Lord, at Damascus, which is a very fair and rich city, and full of all manner of merchandise ; and I have been by Byzantium, and have seen all the holy relics there kept ; to wit, the cross of our Lord, and His coat, and the sponge and reed wherewith the heathen Jews ['Cursed be they !' interposed Friar Andrew] did give Him to drink, and more blessed relics else than I have the time to write of, the which nathless be named, as I think, in the Travels of Sir John Maundeville. This city of Damascus is very great, and there be about the same so fair gardens as I never did see at any other place ; moreover, Saint Paul here dwelt, and was a leech.[1] Also I give you to wit, good lady, that I look by our Lord's help, to go on to the holy city of Jerusalem, the which is from here five days' journey. And I send you herein a fine piece of baudekyn, the bravest I could see, the which I bought in the market at Byzantium, to make you a rare gown for feast-

---

[1] The reader does not need to search through the Acts of the Apostles for any mention of Saint Paul's having been a doctor for it is one of the endless legends of the Middle Ages, of which Maundeville's Travels are full.

days. Moreover, I beseech you to say unto good
Father Andrew, (I count he will read this letter, and
therefore do say unto himself), I would fain have
sent you somewhat likewise, good father, but as yet
I found not to my hand aught that would like you ;
but I look, when I shall be in Jerusalem, if it be the
Lord's pleasure that I come therein, for to get you
some relics, by the which I wis you will set great
store. ['Thou art a good lad,' said the friar].

"Edmund Carew is in health, and is a faithful
squire, and a passing honest fellow ; [1] but he doth
long for to hear news of his father, and my heart
also is ofttimes sore to wit what is become of mine
old friend. If you shall hear of any one who wendeth
unto the Land of Promise, I beseech you send us news
herein. Likewise would I fain know somewhat of
the Lord Marnell, who I guess [2] hath now returned
to London. Is Geoffrey yet with you ? I pray you
ask him if he remembereth me, for an' he doth, I
will bring him a brave thing when I shall come :
and God's blessing and mine be with the sweet heart,
and keep him ever from all evil.

[1] A very pleasant companion. "Fellow" and "companion"
have now exchanged meanings, though we still speak of a bed-
fellow and the *fellow* to a glove.

[2] This "Americanism" is really an old English phrase, as many
more so-called Americanisms also are.

"I beseech you commend me humbly unto the Lord Marnell, if you see him or send to him, and also unto Sir Ralph Marston, when you shall have speech of him; and greet well all the maidens and servants from me. Pray salute also Mistress Katherine on my part, and specially Mistress Alice Jordan. Moreover, I beseech you to make my most humble duty and service unto my good knight my father, and my good lady my mother, and salute from me lovingly my sistren, who I trust be all in health. I met this holy Palmer at a church called Our Lady of Sardenak, the which is five miles from this city; and he hath promised me for to deliver my letters with safety, and in all convenient haste. I have written also unto my father by him; wherefore, if he come unto you first, as I count he will do, I pray you for my sake to put him in the way to Pynsonlee.

"I give you to wit also, good mistress, that in this country be some men who call themselves Jacobites,—to wit, disciples of Saint James,—and they be right Lollards, holding that a man should make confession to God and no wise unto the priest; and also read they God's Word in their own tongue, and not in Latin, the which giveth me much marvel how they came in this place, for they do wit nothing of us and of our country. Nathless, I trow that God learneth[1] His own alike in all lands and at divers times.

"I pray you specially, good mistress, that you give me to wit how I may come home. Doth King Henry still reign? and is he yet evil affected toward the Lollards? for so long as things be in this case, I dare in no wise take my way unto you.

"And now, dear mistress, I pray God to have you in His holy keeping, to the which I commit you all.

"From your very humble serving-man and loving friend,   RICHARD PYNSON.

"Edmund Carew prayeth me for to make his lowly commendations unto you.

"Written at Damascus, this xxvii day of November."

This was the first and last letter which Dame Lovell received from Richard Pynson. Probably he wrote many others, but they never came to hand.

Friar Andrew, with the greatest difficulty, managed to write back a few lines. His letter took him a whole week to compose and transfer to paper. It was written in short sentences, like a child's epistle; and nearly every sentence commenced with Richard's name. Friar Andrew informed his correspondent that

---

[1] Teaches.

all parties named in his letter were well ; that Geoffrey was still with them, sent his loving commendations, and said he remembered him, and would never forget him as long as he lived ; that of Lord Marnell they had only heard a rumour which they could not believe, of his having joined an insurrection in the West ; that Master Carew was had up to London and strictly examined by the council, but that his answers were so ingeniously evasive that they could lay hold of nothing, and nothing had been found in his house which could criminate him ; he had accordingly been dismissed with a caution. Sir Ralph Marston had privately declared that " the old fox must have hidden his Lollard books in some uncommonly safe place, for I wis he had some." Friar Andrew concluded his letter with a malediction upon " evil companions," by which he meant the anti-Lollard party ; for though Andrew cared not a straw about the matter of opinion, he could never forgive them for his favourite's death. He also besought Richard to " look well to his ways, and have nought to do with heathen Jews and Saracens, who all worshipped mawmetis," [1] and to come home

---

[1] Idols. Our forefathers had a rooted idea that Jews and Mohammedans were idolaters. Their very word for idols, " Mawmetis," was a corruption of the name of Mahomet.

as soon as he could—which, however, must not be just now.

Friar Andrew then folded his elaborate and arduous piece of composition, and directed it in remarkable characters and singular spelling, as follows :—

" *To y* *hondes of y* *veraye gode Knyghte, Syr Rechurt Pynsone of Pinnsonnle, beyng yn y* *Halie Londe at Dommosscsc* (this word gave him immense trouble), *or elsewhar, dilyuher thes.*"

" There ! " said the friar, with a deep sigh of relief in conclusion, as he exhibited the fruit of his prowess in triumph to Dame Lovell. " Methinketh that Richard himself could not better those letters ! "

Dame Lovell looked with unfeigned admiration at the cabalistic characters, for such they were in her eyes, and declared them " right brave," opining moreover that " learning was soothly a passing rare thing ! "

CHAPTER XIII.

THE DAY AFTER AGINCOURT.

"Urbs Cœlestis ! Urbs Beata !
Super petram collocata,
Urbs in portu satis tuto,
De lonquinquo te saluto ;
Te saluto, te suspiro,
Te affecto, te requiro."

FOURTEEN years had passed away since the burning of the Lady Marnell. A new king had risen up, who was not a whit less harshly inclined towards the Lollards than his predecessor had been. This monarch, Henry V., of chivalrous memory, was riding over the field of Agincourt, the day after the battle, surrounded by about twenty of his nobles. Behind the nobles rode their squires, and all around them on the field lay the dead and dying.

"Saw you yonder knight, Master Wentworth," inquired one of the squires of his next neighbour, "that we marked a-riding down by the woody knoll

to the left, shortly afore the fight ?   I marvel if he
meant to fight."

"He had it, if he meant it not," answered the other ;
"the knight, you would say, who bore three silver
arrows ? "

"Aye, the same. What befell him ? "

"A party of French skirmishers came down upon
him and his squire, and they were both forced to
draw sword. The knight defended himself like a
gallant knight, but—our Lady aid us !—they were
twelve to two, or thereabouts : it was small marvel
that he fell."

"He did fall ?   And the squire ? "

"The squire fought so bravely, that he earned well
his gilded spurs. [1] He stood over his master where
he fell, and I trow the French got not his body so
long as the squire was alive ; but I saw not the end
of it, for my master bade me thence."

"I pray you," interposed a third squire, "wit you
who is yon youth that rideth by the King's left hand ? "

"The tall, pale, fair-haired youth on the white
horse ? "

"He."

"That is the Lord Marnell—a new favourite."

[1] Gilded spurs were the mark of a knight.

" The Lord Marnell ! Is he a kinsman of the Lady Marnell, who——"

"Hush ! Yes, her son."

" His father is dead, also, then ? "

" His father was beheaded about twelve years gone, on account of having taken part in a rebellion, got up by the friends of King Richard ; but it was said at the time privily, that an' he had not been suspected of Lollardism, his part in the rebellion might have been forgiven."

"Where, then, dwelt this youth, his son ? "

" In the North, I ween, somewhere, with his grand-mother, who hath died not long since. Then the young Lord came down to seek his fortune in London and the King's Grace saw him, and fancied him."

The squires' conversation, and themselves as well, came to a sudden stop, for the King and his suite had halted in front of them.

Almost in their way, on the ground lay a wounded man. His visor was raised, and his face visible ; but his surcoat was slashed and covered with mire and blood, so that the eye could no longer discern the device embroidered on it. A scallop-shell fastened to his helmet, intimated that he had at some past time been a pilgrim to the shrine of Saint James of

Compostella; while the red cross upon his shoulder was an indisputable indication that he "came from the East Countrie." His age would have been difficult to guess. It did not seem to be years which had blanched the hair and beard, and had given to the face a wearied, travel-worn look—a look which so changed the countenance from what it might otherwise have been, that even

> "——The mother that him bare,
> If she had been in presence there,
> She had not known her child." [1]

Close to the dying man lay, apparently, his squire—dead; and beside him was a shield, turned with its face to the ground.

"The very same knight whom we saw a-riding down the knoll!" said one of the squires, with an oath. A man was thought very pious in the fourteenth and fifteenth centuries if he did not swear pretty freely. "At least I ween it be the same—I should wit well the shield an' I could see it."

King Henry and his nobles were attentively contemplating the wounded knight.

"Light down, my Lord Marnell," said the King, "and see what is the device upon yon shield. We

[1] Marmion.

would know which of our faithful servants we have unhappily lost."

As the King spoke, the eyes of the dying man suddenly turned to Geoffrey Marnell, who sprang lightly from his horse to fulfil the royal order. He knelt down by the shield, and lifted it up to examine the arms; and as he turned it, the well-known cognisance of Pynson of Pynsonlee—the three silver arrows—met his eye. An exclamation of mingled sorrow and surprise burst from Geoffrey's lips.

" Who is he ? " said Henry, eagerly.

" Sir Richard Pynson of Pynsonlee, an't please your Grace."

" Ha ! the Lollard knight ! " cried the King. " Better he than another ! I had bruit of him, and, truly, I looked to have him to the stake when he should return from his Eastern travel. It is well."

The King and his suite rode on ; but Geoffrey was not one of them. He had thrown down the shield, and had turned to the dear friend of his youth, who lay dying before him.

" Richard ! dear, dear Richard ! " he said, in trembling accents. " How came you here ? Have you only come home to die ? O Richard, die not just now ! But perchance it were better so," he added, in a low tone, recalling the cruel words of the King. " Is it thus that thy God hath granted thee that which thou requestedst, and hath not let thee pass through the fiery trial ? "

As Geoffrey thus bemoaned the fate of his old friend, he fancied that he saw Richard's lips move, and he bent his head low to catch his last words. Faintly, but audibly, those two last words, so full of meaning, reached his ear. And the first of the two was " Margery ! " and the last " Jesus ! "

The tears fell from Geoffrey's eyes, as he softly kissed the pale brow of the dead ; and then, remounting his horse, he galloped after the King. There was no need of his remaining longer ; for he could do nothing more for Richard Pynson, when he had clasped hands with Margery Lovell at the gates of the *Urbs Beata.*

THE END.

www.ingramcontent.com/pod-product-compliance
Lightning Source LLC
Chambersburg PA
CBHW030846270326
41928CB00007B/1245